PUT ON THE FULL ARMOR OF GOD

The Demands of Spiritual Warfare

BRENT COLLOWAY &
EDWARD D. ANDREWS

PUT ON THE FULL ARMOR OF GOD

The Demands of Spiritual Warfare

Brent Calloway & Edward D. Andrews

Christian Publishing House

Cambridge, Ohio

PUT ON THE FULL ARMOR OF GOD: The Demands of Spiritual Warfare Brent Calloway & Edward D. Andrews

ISBN-13: 978-1-949586-70-1

ISBN-10: 1-949586-70-7

Table of Contents

INTRODUCTION Whole Armor of God 7

EPHESIANS 6:10 15

EPHESIANS 6:11 27

EPHESIANS 6:12 34

EPHESIANS 6:13 44

EPHESIANS 6:14 49

EPHESIANS 6:15 59

EPHESIANS 6:16 63

EPHESIANS 6:17 69

EPHESIANS 6:18 80

EPHESIANS 6:19 84

The Need to Be Bold 85

What Was the Reason for the Direct and Supernatural Work of the Holy Spirit in the First Century? 88

What Were the Gifts of the Holy Spirit in the First-Century? 89

Convicting the World Concerning Sin 91

The Work of the Holy Spirit in the First Century 93

As for Tongues, They Will Cease 93

The Holy Spirit and Today's Christians 100

Obtain Boldness 103

EPHESIANS 6:20 108

Using God's Word with Persuasion 108

Carry on Using God's Word Skillfully 110

Defending the Hope That Is In You 110

Using the Bible to Defend Our Hope 114

The Third Obstacle to Our Being an Effective Evangelist 116

Threefold Assistance in Our Being an Effective Evangelist 117

On what Foundation Should Our Evangelism Be Based? 121

Using God's Word Skillfully 122

Apollos Speaks Boldly in Ephesus............................125

Helping Spiritually 125

Bibliography..129

INTRODUCTION Whole Armor of God

By Edward D. Andrews

Ephesians 6:10-20 Updated American Standard Version (UASV)

[10] Finally, be strong in the Lord and in the strength of his might. [11] Put on the full armor of God, so that you will be able to stand firm against the schemes of the devil. [12] For our wrestling[1] is not against flesh and blood, but against the rulers, against the powers, against the world-rulers of this darkness, against the wicked spirit forces in the heavenly places.

[13] Therefore, take up the whole armor[2] of God, so that you will be able to resist in the evil day, and having done everything, to stand firm. [14] Stand firm, therefore, with your loins **girded**[3] **about with truth**, and having put on **the breastplate of righteousness,** [15] and with **your feet shod with the preparation of the gospel** of peace; [16] in all things, taking up **the shield of faith** with which you will be able to extinguish all the flaming arrows of the evil one. [17] And take the **helmet of salvation**, and the **sword of the Spirit**, which is the word of God.

[18] Through **all prayer and petition** praying at all times in the Spirit, and with this in view, keep awake with all perseverance and making supplication for all the holy ones. [19] Pray also for me, that the words may be given to me when I open my mouth, so that I may be able to speak boldly in making known the mystery[4] of the gospel, [20] for which I am an ambassador in chains;[5] that in it I may speak boldly, as I ought to speak.

You may be thinking that it seems very unlikely that any human can be at odds with a demonic spirit creature and come out victorious as they have unimaginable superhuman abilities. It is only possible by our reliance

---

[1] Or struggle

[2] **Armor:** (Heb. *keli*; Gr. *panoplia*) The weapons and armor worn by soldiers used in fighting, which makes up the whole of his offensive and defensive equipment. This would include a helmet to protect the head, the girdle, and a leather belt worn around the waist or hips to protect the loins, the breastplate to protect vital organs, especially the heart. It also included a coat of mail, i.e., scale body armor for protection during battle, greaves, namely shin guards, and the shield, usually carried on the left arm or in the left hand. – 1 Sam. 7:5-6; 31:9; Eph. 6:13-17.

[3] (an idiom, literally 'to gird up the loins') to cause oneself to be in a state of readiness–'to get ready, to prepare oneself.'

[4] **Mystery; Secret:** (Gr. *mystērion*) A sacred divine mystery or secret doctrine that lies with God alone, which is withheld from both the angelic body and humans, until the time he determines that it is to be revealed, and to those to whom he chooses to make it known.– Mark 4:11; Rom. 11:25; 16:25; 1 Cor. 2:1; 4:1; 13:2; 14:2; 15:51; Eph. 1:9; 6:19; Col. 1:26; 2:2; 2 Thess. 2:7; 1 Tim. 3:9; Rev. 17:5.

[5] Lit *a chain*

on Christ Jesus. We must have a complete grasp of God's Word and apply it in a balanced manner in our lives each day. Only by doing so, can we be freed from the bodily, moral, emotional and mental harm that those under demonic or satanic control have gone through. – Ephesians 6:11; James 4:7.

Defending the Loins, the Breast, and the Feet

Girding Your Loins with Truth

The loins are the area on each side of the backbone of a human between the ribs and hips. At the time, that the Apostle Paul wrote this to the Ephesians, soldiers wore a belt or girdle-like you see in the image of Roman soldiers. It was 2 to 6 inches in width. This belt served a double duty: (1) to protect the soldier's loins, (2) but it also served as a support for his sword. When a soldier girded up his loins, this meant he was getting ready to go into battle. This soldier and his belt served as the perfect analogy, of how a Christian is to put on the belt of biblical truth, to protect his life. The truths of Scripture should be pulled tight around us, helping us to live a life that is reflective of that truth. Thus, we can use that Bible truth to defend the faith, contend for the faith, and save those who doubt. (1 Pet. 3:15, Jude 3, 21-22) If we are to accomplish these tasks, we will have to study the Bible carefully and consider its contents. Prophetically, it was said of Jesus, "your law is within my heart." (Ps. 40:8) If Jesus came under attack by the enemy of truth, he was able to refer to biblical truth from memory. – Matthew 19:3-6; 22:23-32.

Isaiah 30:20-21 Updated American Standard Version (UASV)

20 And though Jehovah[6] give you the bread of distress and the water of oppression, yet your Teacher[7] will no longer hide himself, but your eyes shall behold your Teacher. 21 And your ears shall hear a word behind you, saying, "This is the way, walk in it," when you turn to the right or when you turn to the left.

Breastplate of Righteousness

The breastplate of the soldier was a piece of armor that covered the chest, protecting one of the most important organs, the heart. As all Christians likely know, we have a figurative heart, which is our inner

---

6 One of 134 scribal changes from *YHWH* to *Adhonai*.
7 Lit *your teachers*. The Hebrew verb is plural to denote grandeur or excellence.

person, and it needs special protection because it leans toward wrongdoing. (Gen. 8:21) For this reason, we must cultivate a love for God's Word and the standards and values that lie within. (Ps. 119:97, 105) Our love for the Word of God should be to such a depth that we would reject "the desires of the flesh and the desires of the eyes and pride of life." (1 Jn. 2:15-17) In addition, once we have developed such a desire for right over wrong, we will be able to avoid paths that would have otherwise led us to a ruination. (Ps. 119:99-101; Am. 5:15) Our greatest example in everything, Jesus Christ, evidenced this to such an extent that Paul could say, "You have loved righteousness and hated wickedness."–Hebrews 1:9.

Shod Your Feet with the Preparation of the Gospel of Peace

Roman soldiers needed suitable footwear, which (1) kept their footing sure in battle, and (2) allowed them to march some 20 miles during a campaign while wearing or carrying some 60 pounds of armor and equipment. Thus, Paul's ongoing analogy of the armor of a Roman soldier was right on target, as the appropriate footwear for the readiness of a Christian minister active in spreading the gospel message is even more important. Paul shows the importance again in his letters to the Roman congregation. There he asks how will the people get to know God if the Christian is not willing and ready to bring it to him, as he preaches and teaches? – Romans 10:13-15.

Once again, we must look to our example Jesus Christ, as he says to the Roman Governor Pontius Pilate, "For this purpose I was born and for this purpose I have come into the world, to bear witness to the truth. Everyone who is of the truth listens to my voice." For three and a half years, Jesus walked throughout the land of Palestine, preaching to all who would listen, giving the ministry top priority in his life. (John 4:5-34; 18:37) If we, like Jesus, are eager to declare the good news, we will find many opportunities to share it with others. In addition, our being absorbed in our ministry will help keep us spiritually strong. – Acts 18:5.

The Shield of Faith, the Helmet of Salvation, and the Sword of the Spirit

Thureon is the Greek word rendered "shield," which actually refers to a shield that was "large and oblong, protecting every part of the soldier; the word is used metaphorically for faith."[8] This shield of faith would and will protect the Christian from the "the fiery darts of the evil one." In

---

[8] W. E. Vine, Merrill F. Unger and William White, Jr., vol. 2, Vine's Complete Expository Dictionary of Old and New Testament Words (Nashville, TN: T. Nelson, 1996), 571.

ancient times, the darts[9] of the soldiers were often hollowed out having small iron receptacles, which were filled with a clear colorless flammable mixture of light hydrocarbons that burned. This was one of the most lethal weapons as it caused havoc among the enemy troops unless the soldiers had the large body shields that had been drenched in water and could quench the fiery darts. In fact, the earliest manuscripts repeat the definite article, literally "the darts of the evil one, the fiery (darts)," emphasizing the fact that they were, above all, destructive. If the soldier's shield caught fire, he would be tempted to throw it down, leaving himself open to the enemy's spear.

What does the highly metaphorical language of the fiery darts depict and how does this weaken or undercut our faith? It may come in the form of minor persecution if we live in the Western world, such as being ridiculed for our Christian faith, even verbally assaulted by Bible critics. Another fiery dart may be the temptation to put money over the ministry. Then, there is the constant temptation from Satan's world to lure us into immorality. You would have to be literally blindfolded to not see sexually-explicit images hundreds of times per day, as it is used to sell everything. It is not only the images but also the mindset. I will give you just one example, and please excuse the graphic nature. The modern-day junior high school children (13 and 14 years old); literally view oral sex as being no different than kissing one another on the lips.

If we are to protect our Christian family, our congregation of brothers and sisters, and ourselves, we must possess **"the shield of faith."** Faith is not a mere belief in Jesus Christ as some misinformed ones might tell us; rather it is an active faith in Jesus Christ. James says at 1:19 "You believe that God is one; you do well. Even the demons believe, and shudder!" The demons and Satan believe in the existence of Jesus Christ, and yet this brings them no salvation whatever. Faith comes from taking in an active knowledge of the Father and the Son to the point of building a relationship, a friendship based on the deepest love, and the committing of oneself to the point of turning your life over completely. It is regular prayerful communication, understanding and valuing how he protects us. – Joshua 23:14; Luke 17:5; Romans 10:17.

Yet again, we turn to our great exemplar, Jesus Christ, who demonstrated his faith throughout some very trying times. He completely trusted the Father to accomplish his will and purposes. (Matthew 26:42, 53, 54; John 6:38) A great example of this trust can be found when Jesus was in the garden of Gethsemane. He was in great anguish because he knew

---

[9] 6.36 belos, ous n: a missile, including arrows (propelled by a bow) or darts (hurled by hand)—'arrow, dart.' In the NT belos occurs only in a highly figurative context, to bele ... peporomena 'flaming arrows (or darts)' Eph 6:16, and refers to temptations by the Devil.—Louw and Nida 6.36.

that he was going to be executed as a blasphemer of his Father, and even then, he fell with his face to the ground and prayed, "My Father, if it is possible, may this cup be taken from me. Yet not as I will, but as you will." (Matthew 26:39) Not that he was backing out of the execution, the ransom that is, but he wanted to be executed for another reason, other than a blasphemer. Jesus was an integrity keeper, which brought great joy to the Father. (Proverbs 27:11) As we face difficult times in the world that is alienated from God, we will do well to imitate Jesus great faith, and not give out under the pressures of a world that lies in the hands of the evil one. Moreover, our faith will be refined if we trust in God, evidencing our love for him, by applying his Word in our daily walking with him. (Psalm 19:7-11; 1 John 5:3) The immediate gratifications that this world has to offer could never compare with the blessings that lie ahead. – Proverbs 10:22.

Not long ago, those trying to curb the use of drugs within the American youth had the saying, "the mind is a terrible thing to waste." Our next piece of armor of God would be a very useful tool for protecting the Christian mind, **the helmet of salvation.** The Apostle Paul said to the Thessalonians, "we must stay sober and let our faith and love be like a suit of armor. Our firm hope that we will be saved is our helmet," because it protects our Christian mind. (1 Thessalonians 5:8) Even though we may have accepted Christ, and have entered onto the path of salvation, we still suffer from imperfect human weaknesses. Even though our foremost desire is to do good, our thinking can be corrupted by this fleshly world that surrounds us. We need to **not** be like this world, but rather openly allow God to alter the way we think, through his Word the Bible, which will help us fully to grasp everything that is good and pleasing to him. (Romans 7:18; 12:2) You likely recall the test that Jesus faced, where Satan offered him "all the kingdoms of the world and their glory." (Matthew 4:8-10) Jesus response was to refer to Scripture, "Be gone, Satan! For it is written, 'you shall worship the Lord your God and him only shall you serve.'" Paul had this to say about Jesus, "looking to Jesus, the founder and perfecter of our faith, who for the joy that was set before him endured the cross, despising the shame, and is seated at the right hand of the throne of God."—Hebrews 12:2.

We need to understand that the above examples of faith, does not come to us automatically. If we are focusing on what this current system of things has to offer, as opposed to focusing on the hopes that are plainly laid out in Scripture, we will be weak in the face of any difficult trial. After a few stumbles, it may be that we suffer spiritual shipwreck and lose our hope altogether. Then again, if we frequently feed our minds, or concentrate the mind on the promises of God, we will carry on delighting in the hope that has been offered us. Romans 12:12.

If we are to keep our Christian mind on the hope that lies ahead, we need to possess **the Sword of the Spirit**. The loving letter from our heavenly Father, his Word, the Bible is stated to be "living and active, sharper than any two-edged sword, piercing to the division of soul and of spirit, of joints and of marrow, and discerning the thoughts and intentions of the heart." This Word, if understood correctly, applied in a balanced manner, can transform our lives, and help us avoid or minimalize the pitfalls of this imperfect life. We can depend on that Word when we are overwhelmed, or temple to give way to the flesh, and when the Bible critics of this world attempt to do away with our faith. (2 Corinthians 10:4-5) We need to heed the words of the Apostle Paul to his spiritual son, Timothy:

2 Timothy 3:14-17 Updated American Standard Version (UASV)

[14] You, however, continue in the things you **[Timothy]** have learned and were persuaded to believe, knowing from whom you have learned them **[Paul, who Timothy traveled with and studied under for 15 years]**, [15] and that from infancy[10] you have known the sacred writings **[the whole Old Testament]**, which are able to make you wise for salvation through trust[11] in Christ Jesus. [16] All Scripture is inspired by God and profitable for teaching, for reproof, for correction, for training in righteousness; [17] so that the man of God may be fully competent, equipped for every good work.

On these verses, New Testament Bible scholar Knute Larson writes,

---

3:14–15. Each of us is susceptible to this dangerous trap of deception unless we obey Scripture vigilantly. Following Christ is more than a one-time decision or an occasional church service or kind act. True Christianity involves continual dependence and obedience to Christ the king. Paul told Timothy to **continue in what you have learned and have become convinced of.** Our faith is proved by its endurance.

Two elements are necessary for faithful living. First, we must possess knowledge of the truth. Truth enlightens a person about what is right and wrong, what constitutes purpose and happiness. We cannot trust or love which we do not know. The second element is conviction or belief. We express our belief system in the daily decisions we make and the behaviors in which we engage. No one acts contrary to belief (though we may act contrary to our professions of belief).

Paul also wanted Timothy to consider **those from whom you learned [truth], and how from infancy you have known the holy**

---

[10] *Brephos* is the period of time when one is very young–'childhood (probably implying a time when a child is still nursing), infancy.

[11] *Pisteuo* is "to believe to the extent of complete trust and reliance—'to believe in, to have confidence in, to have faith in, to trust, faith, trust.'

Scriptures. Once again he had Timothy's mother and grandmother in mind (see 2 Tim. 1:5). Timothy was schooled in the Old Testament writings and had learned the need for forgiveness, the provision of God, and the necessity of faith. He had also been discipled by Paul, learning Christ and the church. In each case, Timothy had not only been given knowledge; he had been witness to godly lives.

These people served as examples to Timothy about the truth of God, the need for endurance, and the reward of faithfulness. Each person had staked his or her life on the revelation of the Scriptures which, according to Paul, **are able to make you wise for salvation through faith in Christ Jesus.**

3:16. The power of the Bible to affect change and demand obedience resides in the fact that **all Scripture is God-breathed.** The Bible originates with God. Claims of origins carry great significance because authority lives in the Creator. This is why people invest such Herculean efforts in trying to disprove God as the earth's Creator and in questioning the authenticity of the Bible. Admitting to God's authorship is an acceptance of his authority over every aspect of life. By stating that Scriptures are God breathed, Paul established the Bible's claim as God's authoritative Word over all people.

The Scriptures were written by men "as they were carried along by the Holy Spirit" (2 Pet. 1:21). The picture is that of a sailboat being moved along by the wind. Indeed, men wrote the Bible, but the words and substance of what they wrote came from God. This makes the Bible **useful.** Paul listed four main uses of Scripture, all of which intertwine with one another.

Teaching involves instruction. Since Timothy was feeling the attacks of false teachers, Paul encouraged the young pastor to continue in teaching correct doctrine and correct living. The Scriptures must be known so people will grasp their need of salvation and so the confessing community will adhere to its instructions on proper Christian conduct.

Rebuking and **correcting** are the disciplinary authority of Scripture. Because the Bible is God's Word and because it reveals truth, it exercises authority over those who deviate from its standard. "Rebuking" points out sin and confronts disobedience. "Correcting" recognizes that a person has strayed from the truth. Graciously, lovingly, yet firmly, we should try to guide the errant individual back into obedience.

Many times the Old Testament relates Israel's disobedience to God, how the people suffered God's chastisement for their rebellion, and how God corrected their sinful habits. The New Testament continues with stories and instructions, warnings regarding disobedience, disciplinary actions for those who fail to heed God's revelation, and teachings on proper conduct.

Training in righteousness is the counterpoint to correction. The Scriptures give us positive guidance for maturing in faith and acceptable conduct.

3:17. The goal of all this instruction, discipline, and training is not to keep us busy. God intends **that the man of God may be thoroughly equipped for every good work.** We study the Bible, we rely upon God's Spirit, his revelation, and the community of the faithful to keep us on track—obedient and maturing in faith. Continuing in this commitment will enable us to do whatever God calls us to do. Timothy could withstand the attacks of false teachers, the abandonment of professing believers, and the persecution that surrounded him because God had equipped him for the task. God never calls us to do something without first enabling us through his Spirit and the power of his truth to accomplish the task.

We neglect the Scriptures at our own peril. Through them we gain the ability to serve God and others. The Scriptures not only point the way; through the mysterious union of God's Word and faith, they give us the ability to serve.[12]

The apostle Paul stressed the significance of God's Word when he wrote to Timothy, "Continue in what you have learned and have firmly believed." "The things" that Paul revealed are Bible truths, which moved Timothy to grow into having faith in the gospel. These same truths, along with the entire Word of God (i.e., "All Scripture), can affect us today in the same way, making us "wise for salvation through faith in Christ Jesus." While the chapters covering Ephesians 6:10-18 will deal with the spiritual warfare that we find ourselves in, the two final chapters covering Ephesians 6:19-20 will help us appreciate what it means to speak boldly about the Gospel and how we can become more effective in doing so.

---

[12] Knute Larson, *I & II Thessalonians, I & II Timothy, Titus, Philemon*, vol. 9, Holman New Testament Commentary (Nashville, TN: Broadman & Holman Publishers, 2000), 305–307.

EPHESIANS 6:10

By Brent Calloway

Ephesians 6:10 Updated American Standard Version (UASV)

[10] Finally, be strong in the Lord and in the strength of his might.

In Ephesians 6:10 the Apostle Paul is now coming to the conclusion to his letter to the Church of Ephesus and begins his final concluding remarks by using the transitional word **finally.** Finally, Paul is saying that after all that I have said up to this point, it will not be fully understood or able to be applied unless they see it in light of what he says he is about to say now. Therefore, the word **finally** connects chapters 1-6:9 to these last few verses of chapter 6:10-20. If you were to look at Ephesians chapters 1-6:9 you would find that Paul has discussed some very important truths with the Ephesians. In chapters 1-3 of Ephesians Paul discussed with these Ephesians matters in regard to their position with Christ so they would know their identity in him. Then in chapters 4-6:9 Paul deals with Christians in matters of their attitude, emotions, and actions that were essential to their Christian life. Then, when you come to Ephesians 6:10-20 the Apostle Paul is going to conclude his letter in helping these Christians to understand the unseen spiritual warfare in which they were going to be engaged.

It is significant to note the placement of Ephesians 6:10-20 and that it comes at the conclusion of the letter. This is due to the fact that Paul knew that as the Christians at Ephesus would seek to apply what he had written them in Ephesians chapter 1:1-6:9 that there would be a spiritual war against them. It was not going to be easy for these Christians to apply these truths that Paul had given them, but rather there would be a war against them to seek to divert or prevent them from applying these truths into their lives. In the next several verses Paul is going to give these Christians the preparations that they will need in order to fight the war against the devil and his demons as to have victory over them. In these verses Paul is going to show they who the battle is against, the weapons to fight with, and how to fight as to have victory.

When Paul was writing these words, he was drawing his images of how the Christian fights in the war against the devil from the most powerful army of his day Rome. There is a good chance that Paul was chained to a Roman soldier while in jail when writing Ephesians 6:10-20. Paul was very familiar with Roman warfare and the Roman soldier attire in battle. Each piece of the armor that he tells these Christians to put on, corresponds with the exact pieces of armor the Roman soldier would wear in battle. These pieces of armor would have also been familiar to those he was writing to in Ephesus in the first century as well. They would have seen the Roman soldiers walking by them and around them daily with their armor on. So, Paul draws the analogy of how the Roman soldier fights his battle against their physical enemies and compares it with how the Christian is to fight in their battle against their spiritual enemies.

As Paul begins his discussion about spiritual warfare and how the Christians are to fight, he doesn't start by talking immediately talking about the armor they were to wear or weapons they were to use, that will take place in vs. 14. He also doesn't even begin with telling them the enemy who they are fighting against, as that will come in vs. 12. Rather the first thing that he tells them is what they are to be in order to fight and that is to **to be strong in the Lord.** Before telling the Ephesians who they are fighting against and the armor they are to wear, first, he tells them the condition they are to be in order to be able to fight.

Just like in modern warfare today, when an individual enlists into the military to fight for their country, they do not first go straight to war or get a weapon put in their hand immediately. Rather, the first thing that a new soldier will do is go to boot camp. The purpose of the boot camp is to get the soldier prepared for war by first getting him in proper condition, physically, mentally, and emotionally. It wouldn't really matter if the soldier knows all about his enemy or every aspect of his weapon if, in the time of war, they are not in the right physical condition. A soldier's lack of physical condition would cause him to be sluggish, weak and weary on the battlefield and prove to be disastrous.

In the same manner, if a soldier was not prepared mentally through the strict discipline and orders of their commanding officers, they would have a mental breakdown on the field of battle. If a soldier was not prepared emotionally by being driven to the point of brokenness in boot camp, then he would never have the courage in a time of war to fight. Not only this but it would make no sense for a soldier to go to the field when they have never learned to ever fire their gun or load it correctly. The soldier at boot camp learns not only what their weapon is but how to use it, load it, break it down, clean and put it back to together again. This is all done so that at the time of war if called upon, they will be in the proper condition to be able to fight. Bootcamp serves to get the soldier in the right condition to fight so that he may use his weapons properly at the time of battle to defeat his enemy.

Just like in modern warfare so also the Romans also had a boot camp in which to get their soldier in the right condition to fight. In fact, what made Rome army so powerful beyond just their advanced military weaponry and disciplined structure, was their great physical condition which gave them a great advantage over their enemies. This came through the intense and rigorous training that each enlisted soldier would go through in the Roman boot camp, to prepare the soldier for times of war. When a young man wanted to enter into the Roman army, he would begin by taking an oath of service and then usually was branded on his arm the letters SPQR (Senate and People of Rome). This would seal his ownership by Rome and thereby they could begin training to become a soldier. The Roman boot camp much like the American Marines was very intense and strenuous to get the soldier in the right condition for times of war.

They would usually train up to four months and their training consisted of three important categories: physical, weapons, and field service. During their training, they would often practice marching while being fully armed with their packs on their back weighing up to 60-90 pounds. They would practice walking full armored up to 20 miles a day in 5 hours and would increase as they got stronger to 24 miles in 5 hours. As part of the training, they would practice with dummy swords often times weighing up to 5 times as much as the regular sword they would carry on them for war. This was to build their muscle to be able to use their smaller swords more effectively.

Another part of their training they would also be trained in the high jump, running, swimming, vaulting on a horse, build ditches with walls around it, and how to eat properly as to keep in good physical condition. All of these were a part of the Roman boot camp that would ensure the Roman soldier was in the proper condition to fight when the time of war came. Josephus wrote "Anyone who will take a look at the organization of their army, in general, will recognize that they hold their wide-flung empire as the prize of valor, not the gift of fortune. They do not wait for the war to begin before handling their arms, nor do they sit idle in peacetime and take action only when the emergency comes – but as if born ready armed they never have a truce from training or wait for war to be declared. Their battle-drills are no different from the real thing; every man works as hard at his daily training as if he was on active service. That is why they stand up so easily to the strain of battle: no indiscipline dislodges them from their regular formation, no panic incapacitates them, no toil wears them out; so, victory over men not so trained follows as a matter of course. It would not be far from the truth to call their drills bloodless battles, their battles bloody drills."[13]

In a similar manner, Paul like in modern and ancient warfare will first start by discussing with these Christians the kind of condition they need to be in spiritually to fight in this spiritual war. It would mean being in the right kind of spiritual condition that the Ephesian Christians would be guaranteed the victory over their enemy the Devil and his demonic troops.

[13] Josephus' Jewish Wars III, 60

So, Paul begins with telling these Christians that the proper spiritual condition that they have to accomplish in order to war against the Devil is **to be strong in the Lord.** Paul tells these Ephesian Christians what they were **to be strong** as they went to war against the Devil. These words to be strong indicates a present reality in the life of these Christians as they went into battle, but also with an ongoing action. In other words, Paul is not writing to these Ephesians become strong in the Lord in order to fight, but rather because they are being strong in the Lord they can fight. This was not to just be an occasional way to be when they fought but was to be the very means upon which how they fought all the time. Paul then tells these Christians how they are to be strong in order to fight when he says to be **strong in the Lord.** This entails that the strength that they are derive to fight against the devil does not come from their own inherent strength, but rather a strength that would be given them by God to enable them to be able to fight. In others words the strength they were to fight it came not from natural sources and abilities but rather supernatural abilities as they were given to them by God, as he would dwell in them by the power of his Holy Spirit. In the context of the book of Ephesians Paul is writing to those who are strong in the Lord in that they are: chosen before the foundation of the world to be holy and blameless (Ephesians 1:4); Predestined by his grace thru adoption as sons (Ephesians 1:5); Redeemed by blood of Christ through his grace (Ephesians 1:6-7); Sealed by the Holy Spirit (Ephesians 1:13); Raised up with Christ (Ephesians 2:6); Saved by grace (Ephesians 2:8); Workmanship of Christ (Ephesians 2:10); Brought nearby blood of Christ (Ephesians 2:13); Citizens and Saints of God (Ephesians 2:19); Strengthen in the power of Christ (Ephesians 3:16); Heir of Christ (Ephesians 3:6); Beloved Children of God – Ephesians 5:1.

Paul goes on to say that when these Ephesians were made strong in the Lord, then they were able to fight **in the strength of His might.** The word strengthen is a familiar word to Paul as he has already used it twice in his letter to the Ephesians (Ephesians 1:19; Ephesians 3:16). The word here for strength that strength is the Greek word κράτος (Kratos). This word refers to an ability or might to exert control and dominion. The word entails not a strength that is inherent within oneself, but rather a strength that is given from an outside source, that enabled its source to be able to do that which it could not do on its own. So, Paul wanted these Ephesian Christians to know that in their war against the devil they dare not fight in their own power and might. Rather they were to fight in the power that God would give them and thru them enable them to stand strong against an enemy who would otherwise be much too powerful. Therefore, it is important to understand that this strength was not something they could muster up or conjure up on your own might or ability. Rather this is an ability and strength that is given to you that you might be able to accomplish and to stand in, by the supernatural power that God gives as he lives in you in the power of the Holy Spirit.[14]

The Scriptures make it clear that indeed the devil is a powerful foe and powerful enough to get the Godliest of saints in the scripture to fall into sin and do very ungodly things. It was the devil who seduced Adam and Eve in their perfect state to eat from the forbidden fruit. It was the devil that tempted and enticed David to commit adultery with Bathsheba, Noah to get drunk, Joseph's brothers to betray him, Saul to try to kill David, Judas to betray Jesus, and Peter denies him. In as much he influenced the disciple to flee from Jesus in the garden, Paul to kill Christians, Ananias and Sapphira to lie to him, Herod to kill children, Pilate to betray him, Pharisees to mock him, the Roman soldiers to kill him. Further, we can see the power of the demonic realm from (Acts 19:13-16) "But also some of the Jewish exorcists, who went from place to place, attempted to name over those who had the evil spirits the name of the Lord Jesus who Pau preaches. Seven sons of Sceva, a Jewish chief priest, were doing this. And the evil spirit answered and said to them, 'I recognize Jesus, and I know about Paul, but who are you? And the man, in whom was the evil spirit, leaped on them and subdued all of them and overpowered them so that they fled out of that house naked and wounded." Indeed, the devil and his demons are a formidable foe, but for the Christians, there is no need to fear. For whatever power the devil may have can be trumped by and through the power of God. Charles Hodge wrote, "He, therefore who rushes into this conflict without thinking of Christ, without putting his trust in him, and without continually looking to him for strength and regarding himself as a member of his body, deriving all life and vigour from him, is demented."[15]

It should come to no surprise that Christians will face Satan's spiritual war but rather should be expected. Yet when the spiritual war comes the Christian should not be depressed and downcast, but rather they can rejoice in it indicates. The Christians are to not rejoice in the attack per se itself, but more because of what the Satanic attack indicates. The fact that the devil wars so hard against a Christian is an indication of the fact that he recognizes the power and authority of the one who knows lives in you by the Holy Spirit (John 14:16-17.) Therefore, the Christian can rejoice when they are facing spiritual war because the war itself indicates that the devil perceives you to be a threat to his kingdom. If the devil sees you as a part

---

[14] How Are We to Understand the Indwelling of the Holy Spirit?

https://christianpublishinghouse.co/2016/10/05/how-are-we-to-understand-the-indwelling-of-the-holy-spirit/

The Work of the Holy Spirit

https://christianpublishinghouse.co/2017/05/25/the-work-of-the-holy-spirit/

[15] Charles Hodge (1994) *Commentary on the Epistle to the Ephesians.* Grand Rapids: Wm B. Eerdmans Publishing Co. pg. 374

of his kingdom, he will not war against you but will be at peace with you to deceive you as if things were okay. Yet the minute you pledge allegiance to Christ, then you have betrayed his kingdom and thereby declared his enemy, and he will seek to steal, kill, and destroy you. The reality is that if one is a peace with the Devil they will be at war with God, but if one is at peace with God they will be at war with the Devil. J.C. Ryle said that "The saddest symptom about many so-called Christians is the utter absence of anything like conflict and fight against spiritual apathy in their Christianity. They eat, they drink, they dress, they work, they amuse themselves, they get money, they spend money, they go through a brief round of formal religious services once or twice every week. But of the great spiritual warfare - its watching's and struggling's, its agonies and anxieties, its battles and contests - of all things they appear to know nothing at all. Let us take care that this case is not our own."[16]

Yet why does the devil attack the believer in Christ so hard when they surrender themselves to Christ? The devil wars so hard against the Christian on the basis of at least three fronts that include, fight for control, fight out of fear, and fight for revenge. One of the many factors as to why the Devil fights and wars take place is the underlying factor of his need for control. Many of the wars that have been fought in the past and still even today have been inspired by the desire for control. When a nation feels that another nation is trying to occupy their territory they fight for control over their land. When street gangs find a rival gang member invading their territory they fight for control. When a husband or wife feels like their spouse is not spending money right, a fight often ensues over the control of the money. When a player loses his starting spot on the team, he may go to war in practice with his fellow teammate to gain control over his starting position. Control is perhaps the greatest influencer that generates wars and fights. The same could be said of spiritual war as well, one of the underlying motives for the devil in his war against the Christian is a desire for control. Before an individual came to Christ, they were occupying the Devil's territory and fighting in his army. The devil held them under his control through deception and lies and he didn't have to war against them, because they were already soldiers fighting to protect his territory (Ephesians 2:1-2). They were no real threat to him as enemies but rather in service to him. Therefore, the Devil did not have to put up much a war against a non-believer whom he already has under his control. He was able to control them by deceiving their hearts and minds with lies and doubts (2 Corinthians 4:4). However, when an individual surrender their life unto Christ, they are giving the control that was once Satan's up to Christ. In turn, they are no longer in service to Satan to help occupy and keep his territory but now enlisted into God's army to serve and seek to invade his

---

territory. The Devil's hidden anger then becomes exposed and now the believer begins to feel the weight of the war that is engaged against them, in ways they never had before. As a result, he seeks to gain control back of territory that was once his but now is lost and seeks to regain is back under his control. John MacArthur said that "A Christian who no longer has to struggle against the world, the flesh, and the devil is a Christian who has fallen either into sin or into complacency. A Christian who has no conflict is a Christian who has retreated from the front lines of service."[17]

As another part of the Devil's need for control is his based on his desire for self-worship. A controlling person is one that is most often full of insecurities and inferiorities in which they have very low self-esteem. Since they have no esteem for themselves, they will often time seek to draw it out from other people. In turn, a person will seek to control situation and people around them to that they can gain esteem from being in control to make them feel better and worthier about themselves. Control is a form of self-worship and self-glorification in which one uses others and things around them in order to make them feel better and worthier about themselves. Therefore, when the one who seeks control it is a means to get out of them what they want for their own personal gain. Yet when a controller feels like they are losing control they will fight hard in order to gain it back so as not to lose the very source by which through their control they are made to feel worthy by. If a controller is not in control, they no longer deem to be worthy because they feel they can't exalt themselves in any other means except by control. Often times when the controller can no longer control, they are filled with jealousy towards anyone that will get more glory than they will.

The Scripture described for us that one of Satan's many attributes is control. In fact, it was because of the Devil's desire for control that Satan was kicked out of heaven in the first place. Perhaps the greatest scriptural evidence of this reality comes from the words of the Prophet Isaiah in which many Biblical scholars believe is in reference to Satan when he said in (Isaiah 14:12-14) "How you have fallen from heaven, O star of the morning, son of the dawn! You have been cut down to the earth, you who have weakened the nations! But you said in your heart, I will ascend to heaven; I will raise my throne above the stars of God, and I will sit on the mount of assembly in the recesses of the north. I will ascend above the heights of the clouds; I will make myself like the Most High." This has been referred to by many Bible scholars as "The 5 'I Will's' of Satan." Here in this passage, we can see that Satan's desire for control that stems from his desire to be exalted and worshipped. The Devil could not stand to worship and exalt

---

[17] MacArthur, John (1986). *The MacArthur New Testament Commentary: Ephesians.* Chicago: Moody Press, pg. 332

God when he thought himself worthy of that position. The worship that was reserved for God alone, the Devil sought for himself. The devil in his delusion assumed he could actually gain control over God, which only resulted in his being kicked out of heaven to the earth. – Revelation 12:9; Luke 10:18.

Yet now upon the Earth the worship that Satan desired in heaven but could not get, he still seeks to get now upon the earth. He does this by seeking to take control of individuals upon the earth by enticing them to sin through temptation and manipulation to sin. Satan works with the sinful heart of a man full of evil desires to put pressure upon those sinful desires through temptations, lies, and manipulations to ensnare man in sin and keep him in bondage. Once in bondage, the individual then becomes a slave to sin, which in turn leads to being held under the control of sin. When Satan can get an individual a position of enslavement, he becomes their master upon which he can sway and move in the directions that he wants (Ephesians 2:1-2). This type of individual, in turn, lives to bring glory to Satan, so that their lifestyle of sin and evil, exalts the very god of his life that they are living for. When the Devil gets an individual to live under the bondage and enslavement of sin, he gets exalted by the evil done by them and in that destroys them. It makes the Devil feel as if he is god while he has so many worshipping him through their lifestyles of sin.

Yet when an individual gives their life to Christ, it spurns the Devil's jealous fury against them. It spurns the Devil to see the one who once lived under his control and bringing him glory, now under the control of Christ and giving God the glory, that he once had. So, he wars hard against the Christian as an act of revenge inspired by his jealousy and will seek to do all that he gains to regain control over their lives by seeking to intimidate through feelings of accusations, thoughts of doubt, deep emotions of guilt and many other tactics. He will war in these ways so that if he can't gain control back over the Christian he will at least try to harass and torment aspects of their personality, attitudes, mind, and emotions so as to cripple them in their walk with God. This is to make them as least effective as possible so that they will not do great damage to his kingdom and be of little effect for God's. William Gurnell said, "It is the image of God reflected in you that so enrages hell; it is this at which the demons hurl their mightiest weapons."[18]

Perhaps the greatest underlying reason upon which the Devil fights so hard against the Christians is out of his own fear. This seems to be almost a paradox that the one who seeks to instill fear, is himself the most fearful. However, the truth is that the Devil does not fight from confidence but

---

[18] Fighting on Three Fronts (March 4, 2016). Retrieved from https://4streamliving.com/tag/armor-of-god/

fights from fear. The Devil will war hard against the Christian because of his fear of them. Yet he does not fear a Christian because of something that of their own power, but rather he fears them because of the power that resides within them thru Christ in the Holy Spirit. AW Tozer stated "The best way to keep the enemy out is to keep Christ in. The sheep need not be terrified by the wolf; they have but to keep close to the shepherd. It is not the praying sheep Satan fears but the presence of the Shepherd."[19] The Devil knows that he is no match for the power of Christ and fears that name because of the power that comes with it. James wrote in his letter the reaction of the demonic realm to God in (James 2:19) "You believe that God is one; you do well. The demons also believe and shudder." Each time that Jesus confronted a demon they not only manifested but did so in such as way that showed how much they feared the power of Christ as seen in (Matthew 8:29) "And they cried out, saying, "What business do we have with each other, Son of God? Have You come here to torment us before the time?" We see again the fear of demons to the power of Christ in (Mark 4:23-24) "Just then there was a man in their synagogue with an unclean spirit; and he cried out, saying, "What business do we have with each other, Jesus of Nazareth? Have You come to destroy us? I know who You are— the Holy One of God!" The Devil wars hard against the Christian to intimidate in various ways so that the Christian will lose hope in the battle or lay down his armor to not fight at all. All the tactics that the Devil will use against a Christian no matter how intense they may be, are designed to intimidate so that the Christian will be so fearful towards him that they will never do battle with him. Perhaps the Devil lies even to his demons who deliver his lies, for if they really knew how powerful Christ was, they would never even try.

The amazing thing about the Christians who are engaged in a spiritual war against Satan and his demons is that they don't have to fight for victory but rather they fight from victory. This is a promise that Paul gives us here in these verses is that if the Christian fights in the power of God they are guaranteed the victory. Paul tells us the battle plans for success and that is the Christian must fight in the strength of God and the power of his might. Yet what does this exactly mean for an individual to fight in the strength and might of God? It entails having an understanding that when it comes to doing battle with the Devil you are no match and that it takes a greater power living in you so that from out of you gives you an ability to fight and have victory over a foe that would otherwise destroy you. First for someone to be strong the in the Lord entails that they must be weak to themselves, so that his strength and live in them. This means that one must let go of the pride in their heart for their desire to be the god of their own

---

¹⁹ DailyTozer. (October 8, 2012). *Learn the Truth About the Enemy of Your Soul.* Retrieved from. http://tiny.cc/ly6h1y

life and living is in their own power and surrender their will over to Christ to lead him take control. One must come the realization that they are a criminal under God's laws. Thanks to Adam, we were all born sinners, but we also cannot go without breaking the moral principles and laws within God's Word, which makes us a sinner as well. And there is nothing they can do to save themselves from the justice they deserve for their sin. In turn they call upon the name of the Lord to confess and repent of their sin by faith, be baptized into Christ and in full surrender they desire for Christ to be Lord of their life and live a life set apart unto God (Acts 2:38; Romans 10:9; 1 Peter 1:14-15). Upon conversion, the Holy Spirit then begins to dwell inside of a Christian (1 Corinthians 3:16; 1 Corinthians 6:19; 2 Timothy 1:14; Romans 8:11). As the Holy Spirit lives in you then from out of you flows the power of God. Therefore, the power and strength of God begin by submitting one's life unto him, that he may live in them.

It is important though for the Christian once God dwells within by the power of the Holy Spirit that it will be up to the individual to grow in the relationship with God and draw ever near unto Him. The Christian will only be as strong in God and his might as they are willing to cultivate and seek to grow in their relationship with God. Just like a man that wants to be strong physically, it doesn't happen the moment he gets a membership to the gym. Rather if he wants to get strong, he uses the membership to go into the gym on a regular basis to lift, and the more he lifts the stronger he gets. In the same manner the thru repentance and faith, the Christians enters into membership with Christ. Yet if the Christian wants to grow stronger in Christ and his power living within them they must work out their salvation as Paul said in (Philippians 2:12-13) " So then, my beloved, just as you have always obeyed, not as in my presence only, but now much more in my absence, work out your salvation with fear and trembling; for it is God who is at work in you, both to will and to work for *His* good pleasure." This means that the Christian must daily set aside time to seek the face of God through the avenues of Bible study, seeking God through prayer, pursuing God through fasting, fellowshipping with other believers, and keeping accountable with other brothers and sisters in Christ.

When a Christian does these things and keeps seeking to please God in accordance to his word, then the power of God grows in them and enables them to be able to withstand any attack the Devil will bring at them. In Paul's opening prayer for these Ephesians Christians, he prayed that they would understand the great power of God that dwelt in them when he said,

Prayer for Spiritual Insight

Ephesians 1:15-23 Updated American Standard Version (UASV)

[15] For this reason I too, having heard of the faith in the Lord Jesus and your love[20] for all the holy ones, [16] I cease not giving thanks for you, while making mention of you in my prayers; [17] that the God of our Lord Jesus Christ, the Father of glory, may give you a spirit of wisdom and of revelation in the accurate knowledge[21] of him. [18] having the eyes of your heart enlightened, that you may know what is the hope to which he has called you, what are the riches of the glory of his inheritance in the holy ones, [19] and what the surpassing greatness of his power is toward us believers. It is according to the working of the strength of his might [20] which he brought about in Christ, when he raised him from the dead and seated him at his right hand in the heavenly places, [21] far above all rule and authority and power and dominion, and every name that is named, not only in this age but also in the one to come. [22] And he put all things in subjection under his feet, and gave him as head over all things to the congregation,[22] [23] which is his body, the fullness of him who fills up all things in all.

On this Max Anders writes,

1:15–17. The complexity and magnitude of these truths is beyond the ability of us to comprehend or appreciate fully. Therefore, Paul follows the presentation of these truths with a prayer for our enlightenment. He prays generally that the believers might have a **Spirit of wisdom and of revelation, so that [they] may know him better.** Wisdom involves the practical ability to act on what one knows and believes. Revelation is God letting you experience himself and his truth. Paul referred to it here as guiding one into God's truth and God's way of life. For us it also involves God's authoritative revelation in Scripture. Wisdom then becomes the practical ability to understand Scripture and apply its truth to daily living (see "Deeper Discoveries" for a fuller treatment of this subject).

1:18–23. Specifically, Paul prays that we might comprehend:

- our hope

- our riches

---

[20] Three early mss do not contain *your love*

[21] *Epignosis* is a strengthened or intensified form of *gnosis* (*epi*, meaning "additional"), meaning, "true," "real," "full," "complete" or "accurate," depending upon the context. Paul and Peter alone use *epignosis*.

[22] Gr *ekklesia* ("assembly")

- God's power

Our **hope** is built on the promises which are ours in Christ. We need to know our spiritual future is based on the promises of God and find strength and courage in that hope to live in the present. To understand and embrace that hope in present living requires spiritual progress.

Paul also wants us to know our future **riches**. It is tempting to focus on our present need and poverty. Instead Paul challenges us to focus on what God has promised. These riches may refer to our present spiritual riches in Christ in being freed from sin and made ready for fellowship with God. They may also refer to our heavenly possession of the riches and glories of God. It's likely both aspects are meant. Such riches are part of our **inheritance**.

Finally, Paul prays that we might be enlightened to comprehend the magnitude of God's **power** which he exercised in bringing us our salvation. The power God demonstrated in raising Christ from the dead and placing him above all creation is the same power he is exercising toward us to bring about the blessings which he has promised us. Such power guarantees we will receive the hope and riches. That power is also available to us to make the hope and riches the focus of present life so that we live God's way and not the world's, seeking God's inheritance and not the world's.[23]

---

[23] Max Anders, *Galatians-Colossians*, vol. 8, Holman New Testament Commentary (Nashville, TN: Broadman & Holman Publishers, 1999), 93–94.

EPHESIANS 6:11

By Brent Calloway

Ephesians 6:11 Updated American Standard Version (UASV)

¹¹ Put on the full armor of God, so that you will be able to stand firm against the schemes of the devil.

After Paul had discussed with these Ephesian Christians as to the proper condition one has to be in, he will now explain to these Christians the proper weaponry upon which to fight with and that is the **armor of God.** The word that Paul uses here in the Greek is the word (πανοπλία) Panoplia and refers to the complete armor that a Roman soldier would have worn for battle and make them ready. The Roman soldier needed the proper military attire to fight the physical foe, so also the Christian need proper military attire as they fight against their spiritual foe. Yet these Christians were not to fight their spiritual enemy, in the same manner, they would their physical enemy. They are to fight with natural and carnal weapons but rather spiritual weapons thru the armor of God. These are spiritual weapons given unto us by God's divine power, and not of the manufacturing of any man. Paul would make reference to this,

2 Corinthians 10:3-6 Updated American Standard Version (UASV)

³ For though we walk in the flesh, we do not war according to the flesh, ⁴ for the weapons of our warfare are not of the flesh[24] but powerful to God for destroying strongholds.[25] ⁵ We are destroying speculations and every lofty thing raised up against the knowledge of God, and we are taking every thought captive to the obedience of Christ, ⁶ and we are ready to punish all disobedience, whenever your obedience is complete.

John Calvin said, "He means that our difficulties are far greater than if we had to fight against men. In regard to the armor of God, "…man contends with man, force is met by force, and skill by skill; but here the case is very different, for our enemies are such as no human power can withstand."[26]

Paul tells these Christians what they are to do with the armor of God and that is that they are to **put on** the armor. The Greek word Paul uses here for put on in the Greek is (ἐνδύω) Enduo which means "to go in or

---

[24] That is *merely human*

[25] That is *tearing down false arguments*

[26] John Calvin (1974) *Calvin's Commentaries: The Epistles of Paul the Apostles to the Galatians, Ephesians, Philippians, and Colossians, vol. 2,* trans. T.H.L. Parker. Grand Rapids: Eerdman's, pg. 218.

under." The word carries with it the idea of putting on or covering oneself with a garment. In the Greek, this word also carries with it a sense of urgency, as something to be done immediately without delay. Paul wanted these Ephesian Christians to understand that if they were not putting on the armor of God, then they needed to do so immediately, due to the nature of the war at hand. The fact that Paul tells them to put on the armor suggests that this is not something that God will do for them, but they must do as an act of their own will. Paul used the word put on often in his letters (Ephesians 4:29; Galatians 3:27; Colossians 3:9-10; Colossians 3:12; Romans 13:12-14; 1 Thessalonians 5:8), and in each time Paul uses the word it has to do with the responsibility of the individual to be doing putting on. God is the one who supplies the armor, but it is the individual who is responsible to put it on. Another point of interest is that nowhere will you find that Paul tells these Christians that they are to take the armor off once they put it on. Rather it was to be put on and never to be taken off for the rest of their lives. In the Christian spiritual battle, one must put the armor of God and never take it off. A soldier when he is in battle never takes his armor off but keeps it on and near him all the time, to be prepared to fight when the battle comes. So, Paul tells these Christians that they are to be always wearing their armor, as to be prepared for any attack the devil would come at them with, at any time.

Paul after telling these Christians that they were to put on the armor then goes on to tell them how exactly to put on that armor, which is that they are to put on the **full armor.** When a Roman soldier would go out for war, he was armored with both offensive and defensive weapons to fight. It was expected that when they went to war that they were to have their full armor on. If there was any part of their armor that was missing, it would be at those points that their enemies would seek to exploit to kill them. In a similar manner, Paul is going to go on to explain that in God's armor there are both offensive and defensive weapons. These Christians were to daily be putting the full armor on and that they were to leave no piece of the armor missing. At any place where the Christian soldier has a piece missing, this would be the area upon which the Devil will seek to exploit it.

Paul goes onto to explain to the Ephesian Christians the purpose as to why they needed to be putting the armor of God on in that the Christian **will be able to stand firm.** Paul is giving here a confident promise. Paul does not say that if they would put the armor on that they might be able to stand but rather that they will be able to stand against the Devil. This is of great encouragement to all Christians because the fight against the devil and his demons may seem impossible if not incredibly overwhelming. It may seem at times in the midst of the battle that there is no way out or to be victorious in. However, Paul under the inspiration of the Holy Spirit, gives the promised guarantee, that if we fight in God's power through his armor, we will be able to stand against the devil in this spiritual war. The Greek word for **be able** is (δύναμαι) Dunamai that denotes a power that is given from another source that gives one an ability, power, and capability to be able to do something or accomplish a task. So Paul is saying that putting on the armor of God, enables the Christian to have the ability in their war against the devil and his demons. The ability that God gives the Christian through the putting on of the armor is that it gives them the ability to **stand firm.** The Greek word that is used here for stand firm is (ἵστημι) and is a military term that means to literally hold one's ground or hold one's position in a fixed and set position. It entails one having a stable position that enables them to be able to fight and is not a casual standing but literally more like a digging into the ground.

The Romans wore shoes that had spikes at the bottom of them so that when in battle they would have solid footing that would keep them steady as they fought so that they were not slipping, and they were not falling down. In war, a typical Roman soldier was lined in such a way that he was responsible for a 6ft space that he was responsible for protecting not only himself but also the man standing beside him. Each soldiers position was critical and depended on other person holding their ground for their survival. Having a proper stance gave the Roman soldier the ability and confidence to fight and win against their enemy. In the same manner, putting on the armor of God gives the Christian the confidence to know that they will be able to hold their ground against the devil and be victorious in their battles with him. Paul tells the Ephesians just what the armor of God helps them to stand against and that is **against the schemes of the devil.**

The Christian's ultimate battle is against the great enemy of their faith the **Devil.** The name for the Devil in the Greek means is (διάβολος) Diabolos which means "to accuse, to slander." The very character of who the Devil is a slandering accuser and perhaps is the greatest way in which he works upon an individual is through his slanderous accusations. Although many may think that Devil to be some made up cosmic figure to explain bad things away. The Bible describes the Devil as a personal being who is direct and personal in how he operates such as the fact that he speaks (Matthew 4:6); he lies (John 8:44); he works (1 John 3:8); he contends (Jude 9); he desires (John 8:44; he prowls (1 Peter 5:8); he is seeking to take advantage (2 Corinthians 2:11); he deceives (Revelation 20:2-3); he gets angry (Revelation 12:12); he devours (1 Peter 5:8). All of these Biblical descriptions of the Devil show forth the reality that is a personal being in a personal war against the saints of God. C.S. Lovett said, "One hears much about the need for a personal Savior, but the same Bible sets forth a personal devil just as clearly and definitely."[27]

The Scriptures refer to the Devil in many different ways that often describe the very nature of who he is such as Abaddon (Revelation 9:11); Adversary (1 Peter 5:8); Apollyon (Revelation 9:11); Beelzebub (Matthew 12:24) Belial (2 Corinthians 6:15): Crooked serpent (Isaiah 27:1); Dragon (Revelation 20:2); Enemy (Matthew 13:39); Evil spirit (1 Samuel 16:14); Father of lies (John 8:44); Great red dragon (Revelation 12:3); Liar (John 8:44); Lying spirit (1 Kings 22:22); Murderer (John 8:44); Old serpent (Revelation 12:9); Power of darkness (Colossians 1:13); Prince of this world (John 14:30); Prince of the devils (Matthew 12:24); Prince of the power of the air (Ephesians 2:2); Satan (1 Chronicles 21:1); Serpent (Genesis 3:4); Spirit that works disobedience (Ephesians 2:2); Tempter (Matthew 4:3); The God of this world (2 Corinthians 4:4); Wicked-one (Matthew 13:19). The Devil has many different descriptions in Scripture and this perhaps is to his manipulating ways of seeking do evil and willing to take on different roles to do so without getting detected. As a professional criminal is constantly changing their identity and locations so that they can continue to do evil and never get detected. The devil is clever deceiver that takes on many different personalities to work upon people to carry out his evil plans and not get detected.

The Greek word that is used here for schemes it the Greek word (μεθοδεία) Methodia and it entails an organized and well-crafted systematized way in accomplishing evil. In other words, the weapons of war that the devil uses is through well crafted, organized, and systemized means of evil through lies, temptations, seductions, manipulations, and deceptions as a means to torment, harass, devour, and destroy your life and soul. This is exactly the word that we get for our English word for methods which is an orderly systematized way of doing things. In fact, we see that even modern-day criminals who Satan uses as his tools function in the same manner when they commit their crimes. Some of the greatest crimes in all of history happened not because it was just something they did haphazardly or without thought. Rather they were strategically laid out and accomplished in a well-crafted, organized, and systematized way. This is exactly how the devil works through specific and well-crafted manners that are suited to our attitude, tempers, and mindset that will best tempt and seduce us to fall as a means to destroy us.

If you keep what Paul says here about the devil's schemes in context of the whole book of Ephesians, I think we can see the way that the devil was trying to scheme against the church of Ephesus. In the book of Ephesians we see Paul writing to there seemed to be several manners in

---

[27] CS Lovett (1967) *Dealing With The Devil*. Baldwin Park: Personal Christianity. pg. 14.

which the devil was scheming with them against that included issues in regards to: unity (4:1-3), false teachers (4:1416), lying and anger (4:25-27), stealing (4:28), proper use the tongue (4:29) love and forgiveness (4:315:2), immorality and impurity (5:2-4), drunkenness (5:18), wives submitting to husbands (5:22-23), husbands loving wives (5:24-30). These were several of the ways that the devil was scheming against these Ephesian Christians in the first century. Still today in the 21st century many of these things the devil tries to scheme against Christians to get them to fall and destroy them. Today there are still issues with unity, false teachers running around deceiving, lying, immorality that the devil continues to use against Christians today.

Yet the devil's schemes are not just limited to these things we find mentioned in this letter to the Ephesian Christians but the devil also uses many different schemes that the Bible describes such as Accuses (Revelation 12:10); Afflicts (Acts 13:16); Deceives (Acts 13:10); Lies (John 8:44); Hinders (1 Thessalonians 2:18); Influencer (1 Chronicles 21:1); Stalks (1 Peter 5:8); Tempts (Matthew 4:3); Twist Scripture (Matthew 4:1-11); Blinds Minds (2 Corinthians 4:4); Ensnaring (1 Timothy 3:7); Doubt (Genesis 3:1); Afflictions (Luke 13:16); Works False Miracles (2 Thessalonians 2:9). These are but a few of the multitudes of ways the devil's schemes, but his methods will be particularly suited to us as he plots against us. **R. Kent Hughes said "Awareness that we are involved in a cosmic battle that is supernatural, personal, and futile if fought with natural weapons is the beginning of conquering wisdom. We must be convinced of these things if we are to succeed. We must go beyond evangelical lip service to a deep-souled conviction that bursts our simplistic religious shackles"** (Hughes, 1990, p.212).[28] Hughes then goes onto express the reality that **"Seldom does Satan ever attack openly. His strategies are ministered by his devils are nearly always unseen, shrewd, and perfectly tailored for the victim. What are terrible foe we face. He is immensely powerful, imitating God's power and presence with his demonic hosts. He is evil beyond our comprehension and without conscience or principle. He is diabolically cunning. And he is after us"** (Ibid, p. 215-216).[29]

Essential to the Christian in their spiritual war is not just knowing what the armor is but in putting on that armor on to be ready for use. It will only be as the Christian puts on the armor that they will be able to activate the power of God to fight the Devil. In other words, when the Christians put the armor on, they are clothing themselves with the power of God that will enable them to be able to defend and fight off the Devil and his demons. A Christian without his spiritual armor is as foolish as a quarterback

---

[28] R. Kent Hughes (1990). *Ephesians: The Mystery of the Body Of Christ.* Wheaton: Crossway. pg. 212

[29] Ibid., 215-216

going into the game without a helmet or gear on. He would only get hurt and taken out of the game or could face a season-ending injury. In the same manner, if a Christian does not put on their armor on for spiritual war it will only result in serious damage to their Christian walk. Yet it is important for the Christian to understand that when Paul says to put the armor on, he is indicating the fact that this armor is to be put on a daily basis. Typically, when one wakes up in the morning to prepare for the day, one of the first things they do is to put on the right attire that will help them to face the day and what lies ahead. So a person will typically put on undergarments, pants, and shirt to look presentable as they go about their day. They will put on some socks and shoes to be able to walk comfortably. They may put on some glasses so that they may where they are going, or a jacket to keep them warm. They make sure to have the right attire in preparation for the day and be ready for whatever the day may bring. Yet they do not just do this every once in a while, but this is something that they do on a regular daily basis.

In a similar manner when a Christian is to put their armor on in preparation for any attack that the enemy may bring about during the day. The Christian is to put this armor on daily and never be taken off whether day or night, morning or evening. Paul has said that the armor the Christian puts on is to protect them from the Devil's schemes. The word for schemes indicates that the Devil seems to study our lives to see the appropriate means of attack and then plan accordingly. He is very calculated and precise in the way that he attacks that will be in a manner that he knows might be effective with an individual. It is also important to note that Paul did not say that the Christian is to put the armor on to stand against the Devil's scheme as if it is a onetime thing. Rather Paul says to protect against the Devil's schemes, which is in the plural. This indicates the Devil's organized methods for attack are not just a onetime thing, but a continuous ongoing action that he will bring against the Christian. Therefore, the Christian must continually be alert with his armor for any attack the enemy brings. For the Devil never attacks when it is convenient for you, but always when it is the most convenient to him, in the ways that he thinks he can get you the best. When a lion seeks to attack its prey, he does not do it according to benefit of its prey but instead when it is most convenient for the lion. For this reason, the Christian must take heed to Peter's words in (1 Peter 5:8) "Be of sober *spirit*, be on the alert. Your adversary, the devil, prowls around like a roaring lion, seeking someone to devour." The Devil will attack anyone, anywhere, anytime, at any age, and in any way that he can to bring about havoc and destruction in Christian love. The Devil and his demons are ruthless and cunning in their war against the Christians. Therefore, one must always be prepared with their armor on ready to combat any attack that the enemy may spring upon them. Tim Warner states "Only eternity will reveal the number of believers who have led unproductive, frustrated lives and of Christian workers who have been forced to forsake their ministries because of attacks of the enemy. This happens in spite of the fact that the New Testament warnings concerning demonic activity are all addressed to believers."

EPHESIANS 6:12

By Brent Calloway

Ephesians 6:12 Updated American Standard Version (UASV)

[12] For our wrestling[30] is not against flesh and blood, but against the rulers, against the powers, against the world-rulers of this darkness, against the wicked spirit forces in the heavenly places.

Here now Paul begins to show the nature of the battle upon which these Ephesians Christians were engaged in. Before Paul discusses just exactly who the enemies in the battle are, he first of all states who are under attack as he says they of flesh and blood, **for our** referring to Christians. Paul says **our** which includes himself in this struggle which indicates that there is not any one who is not susceptible to the attack of Satan. In fact, Paul himself is not writing from something that he does not know about but writing as one who knows exactly what this war with the Devil was like (2 Corinthians 2:11; 2 Corinthians 12:7-8; 1 Thessalonians 2:18). Paul wants the Christians to understand that the battle that was engaged in was not an isolated battle, but rather was a battle that all Christians were facing, including himself (Ephesians 6:18; 1 Peter 5:8-9). Paul then not only tells who the war is against, but he also states what the war is like in that it is a **struggle**. The Greek word that is used here for struggle is the Greek word (πάλη) Pale which means "to wrestle as if hand to hand combat." This word is derived from the Greek word Palastra which was a huge palace in which people would go to practice and hone their athletic skills. One of the greatest sporting events that took place in Paul's day was a sport called Pankration, which was a combination of boxing and wrestling mixed together in a fight. In this event, two men would fight naked with open fists, no time limits, and no rounds, and there were no weight classes. The only restrictions in their fighting were that they could not bite, gouge out the eyes of your opponent. These fights were very dangerous and at times fighters would be left maimed or with broken bones, and at times resulted in death. Therefore, there had to be a judge who would hold a rod or switch that would be used to ensure the fighters would fight by the rules. The fight was won when one raised their index finger, unconsciousness, or at times even death.

After Paul discussing the nature of the war, he then goes onto explain who the war is not against and that it **is not against flesh and blood.** At first glance, this verse can seem to be somewhat confusing, as if Paul is saying

---

[30] Or *struggle*

that our war is not with the flesh or sin nature, but only against the devil and his demons. Therefore, all of our problems can be blamed on the devil and his demons and never the desires of our sinful flesh. Well when we compare scripture with other scriptures we know that Paul is not giving a pass for the flesh or excusing the sinful desires of man, for he himself said in other scriptures makes clear that man is at war with his flesh such as in Romans 8:5-8 "For those who are according to the flesh set their minds on the things of the flesh, but those who are according to the Spirit, the things of the Spirit. For the mind set on the flesh is death, but the mind set on the Spirit is life and peace, because the mind set on the flesh is hostile toward God, for it does not subject itself to the law of God, for it is not even able to do so." Paul would also say in in (Galatians 5:16-17) "But I say, walk by the Spirit, and you will not carry out the desire of the flesh. For the flesh sets its desire against the Spirit, and the Spirit against the flesh; for these are in opposition to one another, so that you may not do the things that you please."

When Paul says that the battle is against flesh and blood, he is not making an excuse for the flesh and blaming everything on the devil as if he made them do it. Rather he is getting to the source of that which motivates the flesh and blood to do the evil that it does and follow through with the evil that it does. Paul is saying the struggle that we face is unseen forces that are behind the scenes seeking to motivate our behavior and use the leverage of the flesh to entice us to act in sinful and destructive manners. In spiritual warfare, the Devil and his demons use the flesh as leverage to gain a foothold into one's life. They know that the flesh is weak and that it desires to do wrong and evil, so they cater to the flesh through temptations, lies, deceptions, seductions, and put pressure our flesh to cave into their ways so that they can take residence in one's life. Perhaps this is summed up best by the word of William Gurnell said "Were there no devils, you would still have your hands full resisting the corruptions of your own heart. What Paul wants you to see is that your old nature is only a private in the war against your new nature. Satan comes to the battle as an ally of the flesh and launches a massive attack. He is the general who marshals your sinful inclinations, exercises them mercilessly, and sends them out as a united front against the power of God in your life. Compare it to the following situation. Suppose that while a king is fighting to subdue his own mutinous subjects, some superior foreign troops should join with them and take command. Then the king no longer fights primarily against his subjects, but against a foreign power. You see the spiritual analogy: Even as the Christian is fighting against his own inner corruptions, Satan joins his power to the residue of the old nature and assumes command. It could be said that our sin is the engine, and Satan, the engineer."[31]

Paul after dealing with what the struggle is not against now specifically address what the struggle is actually against. It is important to note that Paul uses the word **against**, which is a word that Paul uses 6 times in vs. 11-12 and it indicates a nearness or proximity that which is up-close and personal. Paul wants these Christians to know that there is a spiritual war that is against them directly and intentionally. Paul then begins to explain just who the spiritual war and struggle is against and he does so by explaining that the Devil has a demonic hierarchy that he uses to carry out his war plans against Christians. Paul begins with explaining that the first in the Devil's hierarchy used in the spiritual war are **the rulers.** The Greek word here for rulers is (ἀρχή) Arche which means "first, chief, beginning." This term suggests one who has dominion or has power or control in certain areas. The rulers here indicate for us the reality that they are active in this world in which they exert influence over affairs that take place in the social, economic, political, and religious realm. Jesus used this word in reference to Satan in (John 14:30; John 12:31; John 16:8-11). It seems to suggest the fact there can be certain areas or territories that due to evil activity the devil has a great amount of control and influence there. This seems to be true from what was written in Daniel 10:12-13 "Do not be afraid, Daniel, for from the first day that you set your heart on understanding this and on humbling yourself before your God, your words were heard, and I have come in response to your words. But the prince of the kingdom of Persia was withstanding me for twenty-one days; then behold, Michael, one of the chief princes, came to help me, for I had been left there with the kings of Persia. Then he said, 'Do you understand why I came to you? But I shall now return to fight against the prince of Persia; so I am going forth, and behold, the prince of Greece is about to come." Even through modern-day media the devil himself through these demonic beings to establish his rule and dominance over the minds of those who view them. The worldly system that Satan's rulers govern, and influence is that which is rebellion towards God in the living in according to the carnal pleasures of man through evil seductions and temptations bent towards gratifying the flesh and living in rebellion to God's commands. It was for this reason that John would say in 1 John 2:15-17 "Do not love the world nor the things in the world. If anyone loves the World, the love of the Father is not in him. For all that is in the world, the lust of the flesh and the lust of the eyes and the boastful pride of life is not from the Father but is from the world. The world

---

[31] William Gurnall (2015). *"Daily Readings from The Christian in Complete Armour: Daily Readings in Spiritual Warfare"*, p.40, Moody Publishers

is passing away, and also its lust; but the one who does the will of God lives forever."

Paul continues on in his description of the demonic hierarchy to mention that there are also **powers** that the Christian battles against. The Greek word used here for powers is the word (ἐξουσία) Exousia that means "power or authority, as to act." This word here suggests to us the fact that one has been given the power to be able to act or to carry out or accomplish a specific task. It seems as those these rulers are those who after Satan plans, strategizes, and organizes his attack, sends out as his delegates who actually carry out those commands on the field against the Christians. Paul progresses on in describing the devilish hierarchy in describing that the Christians also battle **against the world forces of this darkness.** The Greek word Paul uses here for world forces is the word (κοσμοκράτωρ) Kosmokrator which denotes one that wants to control as in a world leader or ruler. The word for darkness is the Greek word (σκότος) Skotos which denotes an absence of light and in the context, it refers to spiritual beings that motivate moral darkness of sin and light of God's holiness. So what Paul is saying here is that there are beings of darkness who are evil and being in darkness are in rebellion to the light and seek to spread darkness and rebellion against God in the world. They seek to control the lives of individuals, families, governments, and the whole world through the influence of sin, manipulations, and lies. Paul lastly describes in regards to this hierarchy that there are **spiritual forces of wickedness in the heavenly places,** that are in a battle with the Christians. Note that Paul calls them **spiritual forces,** which means that he is referring to non-human entities that have not human forms or human likeness but rather they are supernatural beings that the Bible describes as demons. Paul describes these spiritual forces as being those of **wickedness.** The Greek word for wickedness is the word πορνεία (Porneia) and it denotes that which is evil, and lacking in moral, ethical, and social values.

The Scriptures also gives other descriptions as well to these spiritual entities that Paul describes as well calling them demons. The Greek word for demon is the word δαιμόνιον (daimonion) which refers to powerful evil spiritual beings. This word is used nearly 63 times in the New Testament and is often used in connection in the Scriptures with idol worship and deceptive abilities to lead people astray to worship false idols. Coinciding with the word demon the New Testament also refers to these demons also as unclean and evil spirits. They are described as unclean spirits 21 times in New Testament which indicates their nature of impurity and defilement, in which they seek to promote in those whom they attack. They are also described as evil spirits 8 times in the New Testament which describes their corrupt nature in which they seek to bring mankind into with their attacks. To sum up with what Paul has said here in regards to who the war is against it is against a demonic hierarchy that seeks to disrupt, discourage, disillusion, discomfort, disarm, disrupt, dissatisfy, dissuade, distract, disappoint, disgruntle, dishearten, dishevel, distress, disqualify, discomfort, dispossess, disturb, disunite, destroy, and deceive and to cause doubt. As Christians, we need to understand the reality of the true war that we are in and the spiritual beings that are battling against us. Dr. Walter Martin said "People who walk around in the middle of a war acting if there was no war are called casualties! And there are people over all the landscape scattered around ineffective in their Christian lives, neutralized in their Christian witness, paralyzed in their Christian activities, simply because they don't realize they are a casualty and they have got to be restored by God so they can get back into the battle."[32]

In the 1500s the Mayan Indians dwelt among the regions of Central and South America and were known to be a very fierce group of people. They held complete control of their territory until the Spanish arrived and took control of what has been called the Spanish Conquest. While the Mayan's were equipped and efficient with a bow and arrow, they were not prepared to fight against the Spanish soldiers. The Spanish were equipped with armor, guns, and something the Mayans had not seen called a horse. When the fighting between the two began, the Mayans had never seen a horse and they thought that the rider and the horse they were riding on was all one creature. So, when the Spanish began to attack, they took their bow and arrows and took aim at the horse instead of the rider. They thought that if they killed the horse it will also kill the rider on top of the horse since they thought that they were connected. The result proved to be disastrous for the Mayans as the rider of the horse would get up and then take aim at the Mayans and kill them. The problem for the Mayans was that they were fighting the wrong enemy, trying to shoot at the horse instead of the one riding on it. As a result, the outcome proved to be disastrous for them. In many ways, this is often how Christians can handle spiritual warfare in that they try to fight the wrong enemy which only leads to disastrous consequences. Much damage has been done in Christianity by fighting the wrong enemy. How many church splits, church fights, and church doors have been shut because of taking aim at each other instead of the real enemy behind the scenes.

One of the greatest tactics the devil is to keep himself hidden while causing you to fight the wrong enemy, in this manner he can continue to work and cause discord and factions. Throughout this letter to the Ephesians Paul has been constantly telling the Ephesian Christian to get along with each other such as in (Ephesians 4:1-3) "Therefore I, the prisoner of the

---

[32] Precept Austin. (May 24, 2018). *Ephesians 6:12 Commentary.* Retrieved from https://www.preceptaustin.org/ephesians_612-13

Lord, implore you to walk in a manner worthy of the calling with which you have been called, with all humility and gentleness, with patience, showing tolerance for one another in love, being diligent to preserve the unity of the Spirit in the bond of peace." Paul would further say in (Ephesians 4:13) "...until we all attain the unity of the faith." and again in (Ephesians 4:25) "Therefore, laying aside falsehood, speak truth each one of your with his neighbor, for we are members of one another." Furthermore, Paul would say in (Ephesians 4:32) "Be kind to one another, tender-hearted forgiving each other, just as God in Christ also has forgiven you." Again he would say in (Ephesians 5:19) "..speaking to one another in psalms and hymns and spiritual songs, singing and making melody with your heart to the Lord..." One of the themes of Paul's letter to the Ephesians is that of unity in the faith. Yet Paul knew that the Devil would do what he could to try to disrupt that unity, and so he has to inform them that when difficulties arise among them that they are not to fight each other, but against the real enemy behind the scenes. Demons were a part of the ministry of the early church and Justin Martyr writing in the 2nd century said "For numberless demoniacs throughout the whole world and in your city-many of our Christian people exorcising them in the name of Jesus Christ, who was crucified under Pontius Pilate, have healed and do heal, rendering helpless and driving the possessing demons out of the men, though they could not be cured by all the older exorcists and those who used incantations and drugs."[33]

We can be tempted when someone in the church, our family, or at work hurts us with their words or their actions. Often times this causes deep-rooted bitterness to settle into our hearts which only leads to calculated anger. The result then leads to retaliation in some way whether through fighting with fists or fighting with words in the form of gossip, slander, and malice. Instead, a better way to fight would be to pray for the person upon whom has injured you, that the spirit that is behind that person would be manifested and dealt with by the power and authority of Christ. Although it is flesh and blood that hurt and wound us, they do so under the inspiration of an unseen force behind them, that whether they know or not motivates and inspires them to act in the hurtful ways that they do. Jesus himself understood what this was like when he had to deal with is with Peter as recorded in (Matthew 16:21-22) " From that time Jesus began to show His disciples that He must go to Jerusalem, and suffer many things from the elders and chief priests and scribes, and be killed, and be raised up on the third day. Peter took Him aside and began to rebuke Him, saying, "God forbid *it*, Lord! This shall never happen to You." Jesus had told his disciples on numerous occasions that he was going to be killed and

---

[33] Leslie William Barnard (1997). *St. Justin Martyr The First And Second Apologies.* Mahwah: Paulist Press. pg. 78.

would rise again, so that man could be reconciled to God. Yet his disciples had a hard time grasping that and the fact that he was not going to establish an earthly kingdom in which he would reign. Peter responds to the words of Jesus in telling him that this shall not happen to him and prays that God would even forbid it from happening. Jesus responds to Peters words in (Matthew 16:23) "But He turned and said to Peter, "Get behind Me, Satan! You are a stumbling block to Me; for you are not setting your mind on God's interests, but man's." Peter's words to Jesus were out of selfish motives and not inspired by God. Yet notice that Jesus responds to Peter's words not by attacking Peter, but rather by attacking Satan. He says for Satan to get behind him, in doing so he is not calling Peter Satan, but rather is dealing with the source of the problem that inspired Peter to speak the words he just did. Although the Devil inspired Peter's words, Jesus knew the real enemy was not Peter but Satan, who was using Peter to get at Christ.

Yet the working of demons is not just limited to the things previously mentioned but the Bible tells us that the demons had the ability to do many things to individuals if not dealt with by the power and authority of Christ in the Scriptures. These abilities include things such things that caused muteness (Matthew 9:32-22; Mark 9:17; Luke 11:14); blindness (Matthew 12:22); self-destructive behavior (Mark 5:5; Mark 9:26); irrational behavior (Mark 5:4; Mark 1:26; Mark 5:7; Mark 9:18; Mark 9:20; 9:26); uncontrolled body movements (Mark 1:26; Matthew 17:15); supernatural strength (Mark 5:3-4); antisocial behavior (Mark 5:3; Luke 8:27); nakedness (Luke 8:27); divination (Acts 16:16); physical infirmities (Luke 13:11); torment (2 Corinthians 12:7); split personalities (Mark 5:9); doubt and unbelief (2 Corinthians 4:4); deception (1 Timothy 4:1-4); incite (1 Samuel 18:10-11; 1 Chronicles 21:1). The Scripture also inform of us the nature of demons as well in that they have a will (Matthew 12:44); emotions (James 2:19); intellect (Mark 1:24); self-awareness (Mark 5:9); able to speak (Mark 5:9) With all this said it is important for the Christian to understand the reality of demons and how they work as a means to support them in the spiritual war. Chip Ingram wrote in his book *The Invisible War,* "Many people in the 21st century might step back at this point and question the validity of this worldview. After all, it does sound a little weird in a modern, scientific age. If you were to say something in a public gathering about the devil and demons, you would know to brace yourself for incredulous stares and laughter. You might not be taken very seriously. But the Ephesians would have had no such reservations. They had seen demonic power. It was a very common observation. The question for them and for us, if we embrace the Biblical worldview was not whether evil entities were real but what to do about them. Paul was teaching the Ephesians a God-given strategy for dealing with something they already knew was true. Our sophisticated worldview can actually hinder us in the situations we confront. We start thinking that the problem is a spouse, a child, a boss, an illness, or a circumstance. These symptoms are easy to see, and I certainly wouldn't imply that they are never relevant. But they are often just symptoms, not the source of the problem. Behind many of the things we see on the surface is an archenemy who wants to destroy our lives."[34] He continues on and says that "The Bible doesn't inform us of this invisible world in passing references or isolated verses here and there. The witness is resounding and pervasive. If the spiritual world of angels and demons is not, neither is the Bible. The context of the world in scripture is just that emphatic. It can't be rationalized out of the Word"[35]

The reality from the Scriptures is that dealing with demons was a regular part of the ministry of Christ, and they came as no surprise to him (Mark 1:39) "And He went into their synagogues throughout all Galilee, preaching and casting out the demons." At times just the mere presence of Jesus was enough to get them agitated and manifest themselves (Mark 3:11-12) "Whenever the unclean spirits saw Him, they would fall down before Him and shout, 'You are the Son of God!' And he earnestly warned them not to tell who He was." In fact, some of the greatest insults came to Jesus as a result of his ability to cast out and demonic spirits as can be seen in (Luke 11:14-15) "And He was casting out a demon, and it was mute; when the demon had gone out, the mute man spoke; and the crowds were amazed. But some of them said, 'He casts out demons by Beelzebul, the ruler of the demons." Nearly one third of the ministry of Jesus was in dealing with demons and Jesus said that one of the ways in which people would know the power of God would be in his ability to cast out demons as recorded in (Matthew 12:28)-" But if I cast out demons by the Spirit of God, then the kingdom of God has come upon you." Jesus responded to the Pharisees that Herod wanted to kill him by saying (Luke 13:32) "Go and tell that fox, 'Behold I cast out demons and perform cures today and tomorrow, and the third day I reach my goal." Yet although Jesus never went looking for them he was ready to deal with them when they came his way such as when: healed demoniacs (Matthew 4:24; Matthew 8:16; Mark 1:32-34); healing demon-possessed men (Matthew 8:28-34; Mark 5:1-20); healing man with mute spirit (Matthew 9:32-33); healing a demon-possessed man blind and mute (Matthew 12:22); healing of demonized boy (Matthew 17:15; Mark 9:14-28); healing a man in synagogue with a demon (Mark 1:23-26); healing a little girl with a demon (Mark 7:28-29); healing women with infirmity spirit – Luke 13:11-13.

---

[34] Chip Ingram (2006). *The Invisible War*. Grand Rapids: Baker Books. pp. 28-29
[35] Ibid, 32-33

Yet this ministry was not just limited to Jesus but was also to be a part of his disciple's ministry as well. Jesus would tell his disciples in (Matthew 10:5-8) "These twelve Jesus sent out after instructing them: "Do not go in *the* way of *the* Gentiles and do not enter *any* city of the Samaritans; but rather go to the lost sheep of the house of Israel. And as you go, preach, saying, 'The kingdom of heaven is at hand.' Heal *the* sick, raise *the* dead, cleanse *the* lepers, cast out demons. Freely you received, freely give." Luke would also record in (Luke 9:1) "And he called the twelve together, and gave them power and authority over all the demons and to heal diseases." As they went out the Scriptures record for us the result of their ministry in dealing with demons in (Mark 6:12-13) "They went out and preached that men should repent. And they were casting out many demons and were anointing with oil many sick people and healing them." Luke records their results as well in (Luke 10:17) "The seventy returned with joy, saying, 'Lord, even the demons are subject to us in Your name." So, dealing with demons was not just a part of Jesus ministry but also his disciples. Interesting to note as well that demons are mentioned in 22 of the 27 New Testament books.

Dealing with demons was also a part of the ministry of Paul as well and often made mention of them in his letters. To the church in Corinth, he wrote in (1 Corinthians 10:20-21) "...the things which the Gentiles sacrifice, they sacrifice to demons and not to God; and I do not want you to become sharers in demons. You cannot drink the cup of the Lord and the cup of demons; you cannot partake of the table of the Lord and the table of demons." When writing to Timothy he warns Timothy about demons when he wrote in (1 Timothy 4:1) "But the Spirit explicitly says that in later times some will fall away from the faith, paying attention to deceitful spirits and doctrines of demons." In his letter to the church at Rome he writes in (Romans 8:38-39) "For I am convinced that neither death, nor life, nor angels, nor principalities, nor things present, nor things to come, nor powers, nor powers, nor height, nor depth, nor any other created thing, will be able to separate us from the love of God, which is in Christ Jesus our Lord." When you look in the book of Acts, we can see that dealing with the demonic was not something surprising to Paul but rather a regular patterned way of doing ministry. We see him dealing with the demonic when he had to confront Elymas the magician (Acts 13:8-12) and had to cast out a demon from the slave girl with spirit of divination in (Acts 16:16-18). In fact so power was Paul in Christ power in dealing with demons that they fear him as they spoke to the Seven sons of one Sceva in (Acts 19:15) "And the evil spirit answered and said to them, 'I recognize Jesus, and I know about Paul, but who are you?"

However, most of the church today has an unhealthy fear of demons to where they will never deal with them or more often than not, they simply just don't believe they exist. In ignorance many Christians fall into the same thinking as Rudolf Bultmann who said "…now that the forces and the laws of nature have been discovered, we can no longer believe in spirits, whether good or evil"[36] On the other hand there are other Christians that can go to the extreme with demons and see every problem as demonic and take authority in Jesus name for every toothache and broken toenail a person may have. C.S. Lewis wrote in *Screwtape Letters*, "There are two equal and opposite errors into which our race can fall about the devils. One is to disbelieve in their existence. The other is to believe and to feel an excessive and unhealthy interest in them. They themselves are equally pleased by both errors and hail a materialist or a magician with the same delight."[37] The Christian soldier will do well to understand the nature of their unseen demonic enemies and be aware of who they are, what they can do, and how to wage war against them thru the power of Christ.

---

[36] Rudolf Bultmann (1964). "*New Testament and Mythology,*" Kerygma *and Myth. A Theological Debate, vol. 1.* London: SPCK. pg. 10.

[37] C.S. Lewis (1942) *The Screwtape Letters.* HarperSanFrancisco: Harper edition 2001, pg. ix.

EPHESIANS 6:13

By Brent Calloway

Ephesians 6:13 Updated American Standard Version (UASV)

[13] Therefore, take up the whole armor[38] of God, so that you will be able to resist in the evil day, and having done everything, to stand firm.

Paul emphatically tells these Christians now to **take up the full armor of God.** It is important to note that Paul says these Christians are to **take up the full armor of God.** In vs. 12 Paul said to put on the armor of God, but here he says not to put on but rather to **take up** the armor of God. The word for **take up** here is the Greek word (ἀναλαμβάνω) analambano which means "to take up, to raise, to receive." The word **take up** conveys a sense of urgency as a decisive action to be taken immediately due to the nature of the situation and enemy at hand. It is a serious call to action to be ready at all times being armed with the armor of God. Paul is telling these Christians it is not enough to just have or know about the armor of God but rather they were to be putting it on immediately. Again, Paul makes it clear that all of the armor is to be put on and that there is to be no piece that is to be missing.

Paul then states as he stated in vs. 11 that the reason for taking up the armor of God is so that that **you will be able to resist in the evil day.** The word for able is here as in vs. 11 refers to an ability not inherit within oneself but rather is an ability given by God to enable someone to accomplish a task. In this context, the ability the Christian has is to be able to **resist in the evil day.** The word that Paul uses for resist is (ἀνθίστημι) antihistemi which means "to stand, set against, to oppose." This word carries with it the idea of being able to hold one's ground, as in a face to face confrontation with an enemy as to oppose them with a firm determination. When the Christians **takes up** their armor and put it on, it gives them the supernatural ability to be able to stand their ground against the devil and his demons. However, it is important to understand that the word resisting here does not mean to stand firm and do nothing against the devil. Rather it means to hold your ground against the devil by active resistance by using the

---

[38] **Armor:** (Heb. *keli*; Gr. *panoplia*) The weapons and armor worn by soldiers used in fighting, which makes up the whole of his offensive and defensive equipment. This would include a helmet to protect the head, the girdle, and a leather belt worn around the waist or hips to protect the loins, the breastplate to protect vital organs, especially the heart. It also included a coat of mail, i.e., scale body armor for protection during battle, greaves, namely shin guards, and the shield, usually carried on the left arm or in the left hand. – 1 Sam. 7:5-6; 31:9; Eph. 6:13-17.

weapons that God has provided by taking up of his armor. It is a psychological mindset and attitude mixed with a corresponding behavior. If you were to wake up one evening to hears someone breaking into your home, then you will do all that you can to protect you and your family. So in order to do this, you begin by being willing to take a stand, which entails you have the mindset and attitude that at all cost you will not back down from the one that is breaking in. Yet you don't just stand there thinking that by just standing there looking tough that it will scare the burglar away. Rather as you are standing ready to fight at all cost, you will also be equipped with a weapon may be a gun, baseball, bat, or pepper spray. This is what can be called active resistance in which you not only have the mindset to stand your ground at all cost, but also have a weapon ready at hand ready to be put into action if need be. Many times, if you will stand and resist the burglar, he will not put up a fight but will rather flee the scene. In a similar manner, the Bible describes the Devil as a thief who was to steal your heart, mind, emotions, and soul (John 10:10; Matthew 13:19). In order to make the thief flee the Christian must be willing to with the attitude that they will fight at all cost. They do so in the confidence they have in Christ who has given them the ability and the means by faith to be able to fight and be victorious. Yet they must not just have the willingness to fight but also equipped in hand with the right weapons to use as well. So that in their willingness to fight and their weapons needed to use they will be able to resist the Devil and have victory over him. As the Christian actively resists the Devil he indeed will flee (James 4:7) "Submit therefore to God. Resist the devil and he will flee from you."

Paul says specifically that the taking up of the armor helps to resist in **the evil day.** The evil day that Paul is referring to here is the specific times upon which the devil and his demons begin to attack. Note that Paul does not tell these Christians the exact time and location upon which the devil and his demons will attack but rather that they indeed will attack, and they need to constantly be prepared. The battle may rage in a season more than others but just because it is not as intense at times compared to others does not mean that the battle will not come back again. The devil will always attack when it is the most opportune time for him and when he thinks he can gain the most victims (Luke 4:13). I agree the devil is clever in his attacks if he can't get you one way, he will attempt to get you another, especially, seeking to get you when you are down. This entails being ever watchful and persistent for there is a constant war against the Christian. George Downame wrote that "The Christian soldier must avoid two evils-he must not faint or yield in the time of fight, and after a victory he must not wax insolent and secure. When he has overcome, he is so to behave himself as though he were presently about to be assaulted. For Satan's temptations, like the waves of the sea, do follow one in the neck of the other."[39] Paul wants these Christians to have a constant awareness of the danger that is around them as to always be ready to resist when need be. Just like a good soldier in the army, whether they are in the woods, or in their tanks, or in their planes they are not slack, but rather they are constantly being on guard knowing that at any time the enemy can attack. In the same manner, the Christian never knows when the evil day will come in which the enemy will attack but they are always ready for it if it were to come at any moment. Again, this is what Peter said in (1 Peter 5:8) "Be sober-minded;[40] be watchful. Your adversary the devil prowls around like a roaring lion, seeking someone to devour."

Paul then states that for these Christians that **having done everything, to stand firm.** The word stand firm is the same word Hestemi that Paul used in vs. 11 which means to stand one's ground. Paul tells these Christians that they were going to be able to stand firm if they have done everything that they have needed that would enable them to be able to stand. All that these Christians should be doing that will make them stand is everything that Paul has told them to do in vs. 11-13. In looking back, we can see that the everything that Paul is talking about here begins in vs. 10 in describing the kind of condition the Christian has to be in to fight and that is to be strong in the Lord. It would be through the strength and power of his might in by the power of the Holy Spirit living within them, they would be able to stand against the devil. Then Paul tells them in vs. 11 not only does the Christian have to be in the proper condition to fight, but also, they have to have the right type of military equipment, and Paul says for the Christian that is the armor of God. Paul tells them they are to put it on and when they do that enables them to have the power to be able to. Then in vs. 12, Paul exposed who the enemy was that they were fighting, for it does not matter in what condition you are in to fight and have the right weapons if you don't know who the enemy is. Then in vs. 13 has told them to take up the armor for the evil day and that they were to be in constant daily awareness of the attacks of the devil, as to be prepared when he comes. So, everything that Paul is saying will make them stand firm, to be strong in the Lord and his might, by putting on the armor of God, thereby knowing who your enemy is and being constantly away of his attacks by taking up armor of God on daily basis. If these Christians were to do all these things, they would be able to stand firm in this spiritual war.

---

[39] A Puritan Golden Treasury, compiled by I.D.E. Thomas, by permission of Banner of Truth, Carlisle, PA. 2000, p. 306.

[40] **Sober Minded:** (Gr. *nepho*) This denotes being sound in mind, to be in control of one's thought processes and thus not be in danger of irrational thinking, 'to be sober-minded, to be well composed in mind.'–1 Thessalonians 5:6, 8; 2 Timothy 4:5; 1 Peter 1:13; 4:7; 5:8

However, the greatest problem with most Christians when it comes to war with the Devil is that they have not learned to stand. Many Christians have lost the war against Satan not because they don't have the right armor on but rather because they don't know how to stand. It has been said that if you come upon a Grizzly bear in the woods that the worst things that one can do are to run, or to seek run at it to scare it off. The best things to do is for the individual to just stand and not move at all. If the Grizzly recognizes you but does not know what you are, they at times will do a bluff charge. This is when a bear will take off after someone running at them but stop short of them. A bear will use a bluff charge if it is nervous, afraid, and feels threatened. The purpose of the bluff charge is to see if they can intimidate the object to make it move and know what it is. The underlying motive that makes the bear what to use a bluff charge is that it is ultimately intimidated by you. As a result, it seeks to use a bluff charge to intimidate you so that you will fear it instead. If it can intimidate you and cause you to fear it, then it knows you will leave his territory alone. If a person finds themselves coming into contact with a bear and it tries a bluff attack, one of the worst things to do is to run. If one runs during a bluff attack then it exposes to the bear what you are, and more like likely lead to the bear chasing you down and hurting you. On the other hand, it is just as foolish to think to run to the bear to fight it, because it will simply overpower you and kill you. The best thing to do is just stand so that the bear can't figure you out what you are. When the bear knows that it can't intimidate you there is a good chance that he will no longer bother you.

In a similar manner, the Devil in his attacks against the Christian will often time will charge hard against a Christian to see if he can see who they are. He will use these attacks to see how you will react to him when he comes at you. The reason for these attacks from the Devil is that he is ultimately intimidated and fearful of you, so he seeks to do what he can to make you intimidated of him. The Devil knows that any Christian that has the armor of God on he is no match for and is an immense damage to his territory. So, he resorts to tactics upon which he can seek to intimidate the Christian to make the Christian afraid and intimidated by him so that the Christian will not stand against him. The Devil has no fear of a Christian who is not in the right position to fight, no matter how much armor he has on because he knows that they will not use it. It is for this reason when in spiritual war the Christian must learn to stand. Sadly, for many Christians instead of standing firm against the enemy to resist him, they do one two things that can prove to be dangerous. One of the mistakes that Christians make when the Devil brings his attack is that instead of standing firm, they lay their arms down in surrender and retreat in fear. There is nothing better than when in war to see your enemy lay down their arms and retreat in fear. This a great advantage against the enemy for it makes them easy targets kill. In a similar manner there is nothing great than for the Devil to see so many Christians never engage in battle, but simply retreating in fear. It is for this reason that the Devil uses fear so much in the life of the Christian to get them to surrender so that they will not fight.

The Devil has an arsenal full of weaponry that he causes to wound a Christian, and there is no limit to his tactics and what he will do. Once the Devil knows which fears work, he will then use those same fears and replay them in the Christians life to keep paralyzed by that same fear, so that they will not fight. There are many Christians today that each time the Devil attacks they don't stand they just surrender, or they flee. The attacks seem overwhelming and too powerful to fight against and so they don't take up the armor to fight. As a result, many Christians are living defeated lives lacking in the true power of God. When the attacks of the Devil come the Christian must have the attitude that at all cost they will stand to fight. Another problem that many Christians have when the Devil attacks are not standing to resist but pursuing on ahead by their own power to fight the Devil. Many Christians have fallen victim to lie that they somehow by their own strength and power could have the ability to counteract any attack of the Devil by their own inherent strength and ability. The Devil is a powerful foe and to fight him by one's own strength without the armor of God, would be the same as trying to stop a lion without a gun. Sheer human strength is no match for a powerful lion and would destroy a man in a matter of seconds.

EPHESIANS 6:14

By Brent Calloway

Ephesians 6:14 Updated American Standard Version (UASV)

⁴ Stand firm, therefore, with your loins girded[41] about with truth, and having put on the breastplate of righteousness,

Paul now after telling the Christians the manner of how to fight in standing firm with the armor of God, now gets specific about the exact type of spiritual weaponry to fight with. The first piece that Paul mentions is **having girded your loins with truth.** Take note that Paul says these Christians to be **having** girded, which is suggests that this is not a one-time thing they do occasionally. Rather this is something that the Christian is to be doing on a daily consistent basis. Paul tells the Christians that they are to **gird your loins** in their spiritual battle. The word for gird in the Greek is (περιζώννυμι) perizónnumi means **"to band, to encircle."** Loins are the lower areas of the back, between lower rib and pelvis, and these are important and sensitive parts as well that are vital. Therefore, to gird your loins is to put something around your loins as to keep them secure and surround them as with a belt or a band. Now in today's language we would say something like put a belt on. When we put a belt on, we are banding or encircling our clothes around our body to keep them on us.

The common dress of the day in the 1st century both for men and women was tunics. The men's tunic was different from the women's in that the man's tunic would extend to his knees, while the woman's tunic would reach down to her ankles. Underneath the tunic, they would often time wear an undergarment called the loincloth or the girdle made of cloth or leather. They would use the tunic for things such as holding money and tools. However there the problem was that their tunics were often loose and could very easily get in the way of the individual if they wanted to work, run, or fight. If they didn't want their tunic to get in the way of what they wanted to do, then they would take their tunic and they would tuck it into his girdle to give them free space to run faster and move quicker. When they did this, it was referred to as girding one's loins to make them free to move. This expression is used by the Biblical writers to show that to gird one's loins means to be prepared for action and ready for service – 1 Peter 1:13; 1 Kings 18:46; Job 38:3.

---

[41] (an idiom, literally 'to gird up the loins') to cause oneself to be in a state of readiness – 'to get ready, to prepare oneself.'

That being the case we need to see what girding the loins would have been meant for a Roman soldier. When the Romans got ready to go to battle one of the ways that signified that they were ready for battle was that he put on his belt. When the Roman soldier put on his belt it was a sign that he was ready for service and ready to fight and it was his way of girding his loins. The belt was essential for the soldier because it tightened the rest of his armor to his body so that there was nothing loose hanging on him. This would give him confidence in a battle that none of his clothing or his weapons would be slipping off him, a soldier couldn't swing a sword if he has to keep pulling up his clothes. In a similar manner, the belt also helped to keep his weapons cling tightly to him, and this would give him quick and easy access to his weapons in the midst of the battle to fight effectively. The belt had special hooks and holders on which to secure the sword to their sides. On the belt was also supplies of bread, oil, and water on the belt when they needed during their long journeys and their battles. The belt gave the soldiers the ability to fight freely and confidence to fight effectively the midst of the battle.

The belt that Paul is talking about here for these Christians is not a physical belt made of leather and metal, but rather a spiritual belt called **truth.** Paul uses this word 7 times in this letter to the Ephesians and the Greek word is (ἀλήθεια) alethea and it denotes the sum of all reality that by which gives understanding to all things. In other word, truth is a fixed standard that defines all reality and by which all reality is understood. In the scripture, we see that truth is defined for us, not in an idea, thought, or theory, but rather truth is found in the reality of God. Isaiah would write in Isaiah 65:16 "so that he who blesses himself in the land shall bless himself by the God of truth, and he who takes an oath in the land shall swear by the God of truth." David would say in Psalm 31:5 "Into your hand I commit my spirit; you have ransomed me, O Lord, God of truth." Truth is found in the reality of God who originated and created all things that could be understood and known as to what reality is. That is why Jesus as being the Son of God will constantly refer to himself as being the truth, because as a man and God in the flesh he came to bring the reality of God to man that they may know the reality of what life is about and it's very purpose, so that through Christ the sum of all reality of life could be known as he was the revelation of God in human form. We can see this in (John 14:6) "Jesus said to him, 'I am the way, and the truth, and the life; no one comes to the Father but through Me." Jesus would say again in (John 8:31-32) "If you continue in My word, then you are truly disciples of Mine; and you will know the truth, and the truth will make you free." Again, Jesus would say in (John 18:37) "I have come into the world, to testify to the truth. Everyone who is of the truth hears My voice." The Holy Spirit is referred to in John 16:13, "But when He, the Spirit of truth, comes, He will guide you into all truth; for He will not speak on His own initiative, but whatever He hears, He will speak; and He will disclose to you what is to come."

For the Christian, the greatest foundation for knowing the truth is the Scriptures which are the very words of God and Christ, as inspired by the Holy Spirit. Therefore, the words written by the men that wrote the Scriptures were inspired by God himself, and thereby are the truth. Jesus spoke of this when he said in (John 8:21-32) "So Jesus was saying to those Jews who had believed Him, "If you continue in My word, then you are truly disciples of Mine; [32] and you will know the truth, and the truth will make you free." The scriptures throughout are referred to as the truth in other passages such passages such as (Psalm 119:160; Psalm 119:151; John 17:17; 2 Timothy 2:15). It is in the scriptures that we can have the full understanding of the truth of God that can be applied to our lives. Therefore, the truth that the Christian must be girding themselves with daily is the Word of God which is the revealed truth of God. Each day that one studies the scriptures and then applies those scriptures to their life they are girding themselves with the truth.

The Christian must know the truth and daily be putting on the truth because one of the devil's greatest weapons to use is lies. Jesus described the Devil as the father of lies when he said in (John 8:44) "You are of your father the devil, and you want to do the desires of your father. He was a murderer from the beginning and does not stand in the truth because there is no truth in him. Whenever he speaks a lie, he speaks from his own nature, for he is a liar and the father of lies." The Apostle also described the Devil as a liar when he wrote (Revelation 12:9) "And the great dragon was thrown down, the serpent of old who is called the devil and Satan, who deceives the whole world..." Paul was concerned of the lies of Satan towards the church at Corinth when he wrote (1 Corinthians 11:3) "But I am afraid that, as the serpent deceived Eve by his craftiness, your minds will be led astray from the simplicity and purity of devotion to Christ." For every truth that God's Word tells us the devil is there to combat with how much a lie it is, and for every lie, the devil tells us the word of God is there to tell us the truth of what is really is. One of his greatest tactics is to strike the mind with thoughts of doubt, deception, and lies that seem to come out of nowhere. This Is to get the Christian to become full of panic and chaos in making them think that the thoughts were their own, instead of being suggested thoughts put there by the Devil and his demons. If the Christians do not recognize the thoughts are being suggested by the Devil, they will accept them as their own thoughts that originated within them and will cause a great panic that paralyzes the Christian with fear. It will be in these times when the Devil seeks to attack the mind with lies and deceptions that they will need to have the truth of God's Word to hold them together. It is through the devil's lies that cause our hearts and minds to often get disorganized and confused so that we lose our footing in life because of fear. It is through the study of God's word and memorizing it, that when his lies come, we can stand firm and combat his lies with the truth of God's word and the application of it. Truth for the Christians gives him the ability to fight the spiritual war against the devil with confidence to gain the victory over him.

For this reason when the Devil comes at the Christian with the lies that they can't be forgiven or their sin too bad for God to redeem, then they need to call to mind the truth of God's word in (Psalm 103:12) "As far as the east is from the west, so far has He removed our transgressions from us. Just as a father has compassion on his children, so the Lord has compassion on those who fear him." Or what the Prophet Micah spoke in (Micah 7:18-19) "Who is a God like you, who pardons iniquity and passes over the rebellious act of the remnant of His possessions? He does not retain His anger forever, because He delights in unchanging love. He will again have compassion on us; he will tread our iniquities under foot. Yes, You will cast all their sins into the depths of the sea." It will be these truths of God's word to hold them together when those lies come. At other times the Devil will seek to attack the Christian with the lie of telling them how worthless they are and prey upon their insecurities and rejection from the past. It is during these times that the Christian can be stabilized by the truth of God's Word when David wrote (Psalm 139:13-16) "For you formed by inward parts; you wove me in my mother's womb. I will give thanks to you, for I am fearfully and wonderfully made; wonderful are your works, and my soul knows it very well. My frame was not hidden from you when I was made in secret, and skillfully wrought in the depths of the earth; your eyes have seen my unformed substance; and in your book were all written the days that were ordained for me, when as yet there was not one of them." For others, the Devil may whisper his lies to get the Christian to compromise and deceiving them to think that God' won't notice or see. In those moments one must know the truth of God's word that says in Proverbs 15:3, "The eyes of the Lord are in every place, watching the evil and the good."

From the beginning in the garden the devil is a liar, deceiving Eve into thinking that she could be like God if she would but eat from the fruit of the trees and all the way then till the end in Revelation, we see the devil being a deceiver and liar. The Devil has had thousands of years of practice to be an expert at his lies and promising false realities against God through his lies. That is why we must daily put our truth around us to stabilize us because the devil will come with his lies to our minds and emotions to get us off kilter and unstabalized so that the can gain leverage to begin to destroy. The only way that you will be able to combat that will be to the extent that you know the truth of God' word.

and having put on the breastplate of righteousness

Paul now moves onto the next piece of the armor that is vital for the Christian in his battle with and introduces this next piece of the armor with the word **and.** This word serves as a connective word to connect what he has just said with what he is about to say next. This word also serves to show that at the same time that one is putting on the belt of truth, they are also going to put on the **breastplate of righteousness.** The Christian must understand that every piece of the armor that Paul is mentioning here may be different in its function, they must all be put on together at the same time. A football player when he goes onto the field has several different pieces that make up his uniform such as his helmet, cleats, pads, mouthpiece, etc. Each piece is vital to his ability to play on the field and has a unique purpose for how he plays. Yet when the player takes to the field he puts on all his attire to be able to play effectively and to be able to defeat his opponent. In a similar manner when the Christian goes to the field to do battle with the devil and his demons, he must have all pieces of his armor on, to have the victory over his enemy. So Paul is going to make it clear that just as it was essential for these Christians to have the belt of truth on, now they must also **put on the breastplate of righteousness.**

The Roman breastplate was made of band or strips of metal or bronze that were tied together with leather, and some made with animal hooves or animal horns that were put together. In this way, it made the breastplate a lot lighter to wear knowing that they would have to travel several miles in a day. For soldiers of rank, they would have a breastplate made completely of metal usually bronze or metal made to fit the shape size of the soldier. This would also make it more flexible and maneuverable during the battle and when traveling. At the bottom of the breastplate, there were rings which served as a means to be able to support the belt to hold the breastplate together. The breastplate was known as the heart protector and it protected the Roman soldier's most vital organs, his lungs, kidneys, but mainly that of their heart. One blow to the heart or in any of the vital organs would be a sure and quick death and the war would be over. Therefore, breastplate was a means to help to fortify and protect the soldier from the attacks of the enemy and protect the most vital parts of his body.

As the Roman soldier needed a breastplate to protect his heart, so also for a Christian they need a spiritual breastplate to protect their heart as well. The breastplate of righteousness helps to fortify the heart of Christians against the spiritual attacks of the devil. The scriptures speak of the heart over 800 times and 600 of those being in the Old Testament and 200 in the New Testament. When the heart is spoken it is not referring to the physical organ that pumps blood through the body. Rather the word heart in the Bible is what those living in the first century referred to as the seat of the emotions. The word for heart in the Greek is (καρδία) Kardia and refers the inner life or person and center being of a man. It is the place upon which the emotions, desires, and feeling of a man spring forth. It is the heart that generates that which we desire, what we think, and that drives our attitudes, emotions, and feelings. Jesus refer to this when he said in (Mark 7:20-23) "That which proceeds out of the man, that is what defiles the man for from within, out of the heart of men, proceed the evil thoughts, fornications, thefts, murders, adulteries, deeds of coveting and wickedness, as well as deceit, sensuality, envy, slander, pride, and foolishness. All these evil things proceed from within and defile the man." Again, he would say in (Luke 6:45) "The good man out of the good treasure of his heart brings forth what is good; and the evil man out of the evil treasure brings forth what is evil; for his mouth speaks from that which fills his heart." Just as the heart was vital for the existence of the Roman soldier and needed to be protected, so also is the spiritual heart vital for the Christian and needs to be protected at all costs. It was to this that Solomon wrote in (Proverbs 4:23) "Watch over your heart with all diligence, for from it flow the springs of life."

The breastplate that Paul refers to like the belt of truth is not a physical one made of leather and bronze, but rather a spiritual one that is made up of **righteousness.** The Greek word for righteousness is (δικαιοσύνη) Dikaiosune which entails "to be just, to do right." Righteousness in the Bible begins with the death and resurrection of Christ, that enables man to be made right. Mankind in their sinful state is an enemy of God and in rebellion against God, in their love for sin. As a result of this, it presents a divine dilemma in that a Holy God can't allow sinful beings into his presence because of his holiness. Another dilemma is that sinful man who loves his sin hates a Holy God and does not want his presence because God stands as a threat to the very thing he loves and that being his sin. Therefore, there had to be a mediator who would come to bring peace between a Holy God and sinful man. Therefore, God sent forth his son (John 3:16) born of a woman and born of man (Galatians 4:4) to perfectly represent God to man and man to God. Jesus Christ by his death and resurrection was the perfect mediator (1 Timothy 2:5) to bring peace between God and man and solve the divine dilemma. Due to the work of Christ, the wrath of God due to sinful man could be satisfied and sin atoned for (Romans 3:24-25) and sinful man could not have the possibility of being made right with God. Now thru the means of Christ, God allowed the possibility for sinful man to be in a relationship with him. In turn, the work of Christ enabled the Holy Spirit to be enacted to work upon the heart of a man to bring about conviction and draw individuals unto Christ in repentance (John 16:8). When an individual in humble surrender repents of their sins and calls upon the name of the Lord to save them, then the Holy Spirit begins to dwell within that individual. The Holy Spirit begins to change the very nature of an individual's wicked heart by turning their heart from a heart of stone to heart of flesh (Ezekiel 36:26). The individual goes from one who hated God to one who now loves God and delights in God. The results is that God and sinful man who repents now can have peace with one another. The finished work of Christ gives man the ability to be made right before God, not of his own efforts but by the finished work of Christ. This can be referred to as the righteousness of Christ because it was his death and resurrection that gave the ability for man to be saved from sin and made right with God.

When a man repents of his sin and by faith trusts in Christ as Lord, then not only do they have a new outlook on God but also with sin. The sin they once love, they now hate and will do all they can to turn from it and live right before God. The means upon which God gave to show man how to live right before him is his written Word. The Word of God reveals the right things of God upon which man is to live by and that by obeying those words, they will live right unto God. This can be referred to as personal righteousness, which entails that after once has been made right with God thru Christ, then they begin to live right in accordance with God's standards from the gratitude of their heart of what God has done for them thru Christ. It is too personal righteousness that Paul is referring to here in this text. In the same way that the Romans needed a breastplate to protect their vital organs so also do we Christians as well need also to have protection over out spiritual organs. They need to have protection over their heart in its desires, thoughts, emotions, attitude, and conscience, because there is a devil that is constantly trying to enter into those areas of our heart as to destroy them and need to have protection lest he does to kill our soul or at least wound it greatly. William Gurnall writes "Righteousness and holiness are God's protection to defend the believer's conscience from all wounds inflicted by sin....Your holiness is what the devil wants to steal from you....He will allow a man to have anything, or be anything rather than be truly and powerfully holy."[42]

The Devil knows that a blow to the heart of the Christian will cause severe damage if not take them out of the battle altogether. For that reason, the devil will come to finds ways to try to attack our heart so that he can deeply wound and paralyze our walk with God. One of the first greatest things that the Devil will do is that he will accuse, in fact, the name for devil in the Greek actually means accuser. We see this in (Revelation 12:10) "..the accuser of the brethren has been thrown down, he who accuses them before our God day and night." This is one of his greatest weapons as a

---

[42] William Gurnall (1986). *The Christian In Complete Armour* Volume 2 abridged by Ruthanne Garlock, et.al. Scotland, Edinburgh, and Carlisle, PA: Banner of Truth Trust, pp. 149, 160.

way to handcuff a handicap many Christian people as to destroy their walk with God. One of the greatest reasons as to why I believe that Satan works so hard at bringing accusations to us is that he wants nothing more than for us to get our eyes off the Savior and onto the sinner. The devil brings the accusations to you so that you will fix your eyes upon the sin you have committed, but not the Savior who took it away. You see the devil is an adversary always trying to dig up charges against you to blame you as to reminding you of your sin and the blame that is yours. Yet you will never find God when he has forgiven you ever bring that sin up again for as scriptures say as far as the east is from the west, he has removed our transgressions from us. If the devil can't find something right now to blame you and accuse you for he has a great memory and will pull from the history of failures and sins in your life as to remind you of what you did. Yet for God, it is not a matter of what you did or didn't do, but a matter of what he did for you. Yet the devil only does this as one of his tactics to control you that you will not grow into your full potential in Christ. In other words, when someone makes accusations it is for the purpose in one way or another to destroy the character of that person. So also, when Satan comes to accuse us it is to destroy the character of God in us and taking it away from us.

The next time the devil tries to come to destroy your heart to depress your emotions and disturb your thinking with negativity about your past, it is then that you need to have on that breastplate. Then you need to at that moment have the right thinking and the right mindset about what God has done for you such as in (Romans 5:8-11) "But God demonstrates his own love toward us, in that while we were yet sinners, Christ died for us. Much more then, having now been justified by HIs blood, we shall be saved from the wrath of God through HIm. For if while we were enemies we were reconciled to God through death of His Son, much more, having been reconciled, we shall be saved by His life. And not only this, but we also exult in God through our Lord Jesus Christ, through whom we have now received the reconciliation." We the devil comes with the lie to our mind and heart of guilt from the past sin, we need be armed with the right truth from the world that says that what you try to remind God has forgiven, and that devil your lies against me don't stand against the truth of the one who is the Judge and ultimately saves.

Another means upon which the devil will work upon your heart will be through condemnation. Condemnation is to declare or assert sentence upon someone wrong, evil, unfit as to cause guilt and thereby doom and destruction. That is why righteousness is so important here and can protect us here against the devil's condemnation. Because here is the thing that we need to know about the devil is that he is very diabolical and cunning in this way. The devil is very diabolical in the fact that when we cave into sin to get us there, he makes it seem so nice and sweet, beautiful, and pleasurable, and then when we get done with our feast make us feel like a glutton that should be punished. He uses the very thing that he promises to delight us and make us strong and turns it around to bring about our greatest shame, horror, and guilt. Where he acts like our friend on one end but then acts like our enemy on the opposite end of the spectrum. That is why when the devil comes to offer sin to us we need to stand and do what is right because the devil will condemn when he has the leverage to do so. So if we are living in any secret type of sin, then that gives him the opportunity to condemn us in those areas of sin, because they are open doors for him to be able to do so. So if when he comes with his temptations and desires to appeal to your flesh to please them, if you stand for what is right to resist them and those sins he wants you to indulge in, then those condemnations that he was waiting to bring your way they just bounce off and they can't bother you no more, when you do right and he can't stab you with condemnations because you are protected by right. Thomas Brooks said in regards "Satan's first device to draw the soul into sin is, to present the bait—and hide the hook; to present the golden cup—and hide the poison; to present the sweet, the pleasure, and the profit that may flow in upon the soul by yielding to sin—and to hide from the soul the wrath and misery that will certainly follow the committing of sin."[43]

Another means upon which Satan will try to work upon our heart will also be through our pride in the emotions. If he can't get your depressed, anxious, etc. through accusation and condemnation then he will go to the opposite extreme and try to build you up and puff you up, so that he will stroke your ego so that he will just make you think that you don't need God because you can be Him yourself. Sometimes the greatest way to affect the heart of a man is not to attack it but rather inflate it so that it will destroy itself. If a farmer wants a pig to get ready for slaughter, the best way to do so is not by starving it, but rather letting eat and get inflated. All the while that it is eating and getting satisfied, it has no idea that it is only preparing itself for a greater slaughter. Pride is the very thing that got the Devil kicked out of heaven and it is the same tactic that he uses to keep many people out still today. It was pride that brought sin into the world as we can read in (Genesis 3:5-6) "For God knows that in that day you eat from it your eyes will be opened, and you will be like God, knowing good and evil. When the woman saw that the tree was good for food, and that it was a delight to the eyes, and that the tree was desirable to make one wise, she took from its fruit and ate; and she gave also to her husband with her, and he ate." When the devil came at Eve he did so as a means to appeal to her desires that she could become like God. In many

<hr>

43 Michael Kruger. (January 15, 2014). *The Oldest Trick in the book..* Retrieved from https://www.michaeljkruger.com/the-oldest-trick-in-the-book/

ways still, this is one of his greatest tactics. That when you start to make that money, get that promotion, people start liking and needing you, get some position of power that you don't need God you have arrived, and then begin to live your life in the exaltation of yourself as you have taken God out of the equation. For this reason, the breastplate must be put on to guard out heart lest Satan strike at it and destroy you.

Finally, another great tactic the devil uses is with manipulations and his seductions as a means to use our desires to his advantage so as to get us to cave into temptations to please and satisfy ourselves. We are already naturally inclined to self-worship and to sin to please ourselves he just uses them to our advantage. So with Peter's selfish ambitions, he tried to rebuke Jesus from going to the cross, David to look longer than should have at Bathsheba, Judas to betray Jesus for greed, and Saul to kill Christians for power, and Pilate to kill Jesus for political gain and favor with people. The Devil will constantly be sending temptations and by which to find open doors of access into which he can then begin to take root into our heart, mind, and soul and cause great destruction and many casualties The devil is like those false websites that say you have won the prize only to open them up and realize they have just infected your computer with a virus. Promising one thing but delivering another. Richard Sibbes said "Satan gives Adam an apple and takes away Paradise. Therefore, in all temptations let us consider not what he offers, but what we shall lose."[44]

---

[44] A Puritan Golden Treasury, compiled by I.D.E. Thomas, by permission of Banner of Truth, Carlisle, PA. 2000, p. 293.

EPHESIANS 6:15

By Brent Calloway

Ephesians 6:15 Updated American Standard Version (UASV)

15 and with your feet shod with the preparation of the gospel of peace;

Paul comes now to the third piece of the armor and that being the feet shod with the preparation of the gospel of peace. Paul begins in describing this piece of armor in saying they were to be **having** their feet shod. Important to note that Paul does not have but rather he says having shod their feet, which denotes an ongoing continual action. Paul wants these Christians to understand that putting on this armor is not to be a piece they were to put on every once in a while, but rather that which was to be put on daily on a regular basis. Paul uses an interesting word in telling these Christians that they are to have their feet **shod.** The Greek word for shod is (ὑποδέω) Hupodeo which means "to bind one's feet with shoes." The word entails being furnished with and equipped with adequate shoes. The average Roman citizen had a couple pair of sandals, some for household wear and others for relaxation purposes and menial tasks. They also had shoes that would cover their toes that they would wear outside for protection from any elements they may face when they go outside.

Some Romans wore sandals that went way up to the calf and knee, so they were designed for more laborious activities such as walking, running, and most had these unless too poor to be able to not afford them. There were different types of shapes and colors depending upon the status and cost, but usually, the slaves and laborers wore shoes made of the plainest and cheapest of material. Women would often wear sandals made of soft fine leather were corked to provide warmth and to make them look taller. They would also wear shoes that were decked with different ornaments on them to make them showy and glamorous. The Romans were known for being nearly experts at tanning and they usually used the hides of deer, ox, and cattle to make their sandals and this would provide them with a thickness as to endure and make the footwear firm. The thicker parts of the hide were used to make the soles of the shoes and the weaker parts of the skin were used for the sandals and straps. Some wealthy Romans used sheepskin or pigskin for style and elegance.

The footwear that Paul is referring to here in particular are the type of shoes the Roman soldier would have worn which would have been called Caliga. This type of shoe was essential for the Roman soldier as it provided for the Roman soldier is that it provided them with the stability that they needed in order to be able to fight. The sandals were designed with hobnails at the bottom of them to keep their soles from wearing out and they would dig into the ground to give firm footing in fight and dig in when walking. Sometimes the Romans would be going thru terrain that would have been wet, slick, and muddy. As a result, they could easily stumble if not firmly grounded and have stability. The bottom of the sandals had hobnails that were designed to give the soldier a good grip in the ground and stability during rough terrain, and traction when fighting.

The Roman's shoes were also important in providing comfort for the soldier as they would often have to travel several miles at a time and at times over very rough terrain. As result they needed to have something that would give their feet protection against blisters, bruises, and cuts. They had an open design on them to have air pass through them to keep the feet cool and also were opened so as to prevent blistering of the feet for long distances. These shoes were also important because they were designed to keep the soldier from getting things such as ringworm and trench foot, and other infections they could have got thru blisters and other things. Also, if they were walking through extreme snow or extra hot roadway, they could have some sort of comfort when facing these things. Sometimes they would travel up to 20-30 miles a day and that which 60-70lbs. packs on their backs and so if there back didn't feel good at least their feet could. It was estimated that the typical length of a walk for Roman soldier was 25 miles and they could do all this without ever getting a blister upon their feet. Yet in winter cold months they would wear socks that would be used to keep the feet warm and to keep the feet from chafing as well. The sandals were also important for protecting the soldier's the feet against the rugged terrain that many of them would go over that could cut them with rocks, twigs, and stones. The sandals also help to protect their foot against the stabs of the enemy as well, and any sharp objects their enemies may have planted in the ground. They were also used as a weapon against their enemies to kick and stomp on them with the hobnails at the bottom.

Paul is going to show us what shoes we are to put on, not those of physical shoes but rather those of spiritual shoes. Spiritually the boots that we are to put on in the war against the Devil and to walk in the ways that honor God is the shoes of peace, to meet the nature of the battle against who we are against. So, we know we are supposed to be wearing shoes of peace, we first of all need to understand what the word peace here actually means. For it is important to understand what this is in order to be able to put them on as to be able to properly fight the battle in the correct way. The word that is used here for the Greek word for peace is the Greek word (εἰρήνη) eirene which means "to bind or join together that which has been separated as to bring into harmony." This is an important word used in the scriptures that are used in every single book in the New Testament. The word conveys more than just external harmony as any absence of conflict but rather a harmony of the soul and heart in which we find a settled contentment that rests upon the individual despite any external chaos and confusion that may be going on. It denotes that the souls' war and strife with God are now over and through repentance and surrender unto Christ one has an internal rest and contentment with God that once at war with him. The Bible describes the soul and the flesh apart from Christ to be at war against him as we can see from Bible passages such as (Romans 8:7-8) "..the mind set on the flesh is hostile toward God; for it does not subject itself to the law of God, for it is not even able to do so, and those who are in the flesh cannot please God." Paul would also say in (Galatians 5:17) "For the flesh sets its desire against the Spirit, and the Spirit against the flesh; so that you may not do the things that you please." The shoes of peace for the Christian is extremely important for them in their war against the Devil and his demons.

One of the ways the peace of Christ is important for the Christian to have is that it provides them with stability. Whereas God wants stability and order to our lives the devil wants nothing more than instability and chaos to ruin our lives. The devil will seek to constantly work upon the Christians through many lies, temptations, manipulations, and intimidations. He seeks to get Christians off balance in their life through the many methods of war that he uses. If the Christians are not grounded with the peace of Christ in their heart, mind, body, and soul, then they will become the devil's casualty. The devil's war is a long war that will be one the saints of God will battle with till the day they die or Christ returns. Therefore, they need to have some sort of stability to help them to endure for the long haul of the battle, just like a Roman soldier would need proper shoes to make their long journeys. The peace of Christ will enable to Christian to endure the daily onslaughts of the Devil and his demons, to be able to withstand and have victory over them.

The shoes of peace will also be important for the Christian soldier as it was for the Roman soldier in that it also brings them comfort. The shoes the Roman soldier wore gave them comfort for their journey difficult journies through rough terrain and through many different types of situations. In our battle against the devil it will be difficult and long at times and will be in many different trials and situations we will face and have to travel through. As a result, the Christian needs to be fitted with peace of Christ to give us comfort through those difficult terrains and situations that will come about in the spiritual war. One of the greatest ways upon which Satan will work to disrupt our lives and to bring about chaos is by speaking to us lies in the midst of adversity. When that disease comes our way, he is there to say he doesn't love you or this would not happen. That loved one or friend or one close to you dies way before the time and he says how could God have let this happen is he really real. When your healing doesn't come the way that you thought that it should or simply does not take it away at all, and he speaks his lies of that he can't be trusted, or why keep going with all this happening to you, just take matters into your own hand you don't need God. When the Devil wars at us in these ways we need the peace of Christ to give comfort to journey through them. Jesus spoke of this is (John 16:32-33) "Behold, an hour is coming, and has already come, for you to be scattered, each to his own home, and to leave Me alone; and yet I am not alone, because the Father is with Me. These things I have spoken to you, so that in Me you may have peace. In the world you have tribulation, but take courage; I have overcome the world."

The Christian soldier also needs to be fitted with peace of Christ as well so that it will give them protection. The Roman soldier needs to protection on his feet in case there were any traps set by their enemies that would damage their feet with sharp objects. The thick sole would protect the soldier's foot from the sharp object penetrating their foot. The devil will try to set traps along our path as a means to pierce through our peace. He may use the trap of guilt and shame to stab at us with the lie that God can't forgive us or help condemnation upon you to paralyze you with guilt and shame. It will be in those moments that the peace of Christ will help to protect against the Devil's ambush in remembering God's words through Paul when he said in (Romans 8:1-2) "Therefore there is now no condemnation for those who are in Christ Jesus. For the law of the Spirit of life in Christ Jesus has set you free from the law of sin and of death."

The Roman soldier's shoe was also important for they could also use it to be able to crush the enemy with the spikes at the end by stepping or kicking them. The peace of Christ fitted upon the Christian soldier is also essential for the Christian to be able to stomp on the devil and hurt him. One of the greatest ways that the Christian will do this is by taking the gospel to the world thru evangelism. The prophet Isaiah wrote in (Isaiah 52:7) "How lovely on the mountains are the feet of him who brings good news, who announces peace and brings good news of happiness, who announces salvation, and says to Zion 'Your God reigns." The Christian must be fitted with shoes of peace that Christ gives that they can go to others that they would experience the same type of peace as Jesus would say in_(Matthew 5:9) "Blessed are the peacemakers, for they shall be called sons of God." When Christians go to the world to share the gospel of peace it is a death blow to Satan and the advancement of His kingdom. However, if a Christian is not first fitted with peace they will never go and share that peace with others as a means to crush the Devil's work.

EPHESIANS 6:16

By Brent Calloway

Ephesians 6:16 Updated American Standard Version (UASV)

¹⁶ in all things, taking up the shield of faith with which you will be able to extinguish all the flaming arrows of the evil one.

Paul introduces the fourth piece of the armor that is essential for the Christians soldier in stating **in addition to all.** Paul wants to make sure that the next piece of armor was to be added onto all the other pieces of the armor that Paul has already mentioned. Again, we continue to see how Paul in connecting all the pieces of the armor together and not one piece is to be missing, but all must be put on together. It would have been foolish for a Roman soldier to go into war and just fight with his shield without using his belt, breastplate, and shoes on. Without having his shield, the Roman soldier was an easy target for the enemy and would have been easily destroyed by him. In turn, if the soldier just had a shield without the rest of the armor on, he could only try to hold back the enemy but have no means to attack, which would mean a certain death. Along with having put on the belt truth, the breastplate of righteousness, feet shod with peace, they now need to make sure to **take up the shield of faith.** The word used in the Greek word take up carries with it the idea of taking something up in order to use. The fact Paul says to take up the shield suggests that this piece of the armor was to be near them and ready to be used at any time when needed. The belt, the breastplate, and shoes were never to be taken off, but to be worn on them at all times in battle and during their marches. The shield they would carry with them at all times but only to be taken up when needed in the midst of the battle for protection.

The shield was essential for the Roman soldier in order for proper defense and to be able to survive. The shield that Paul was most likely referring to here was called a Thureos and it was about two and a half feet wide by four and a half feet high and was designed to protect the entire body. It was made out of plywood or poplar wood double layered for durability, and around the edges of the shield would have been metal to reinforce the shield and to protect against sword thrusts. This shield was usually made of two layers of wood that was covered with canvas and leather covering on the outside and bound with iron. The shield weighed about 22 pounds and there was also a metal knob in the middle of the shield that soldiers used to punch or push through enemies while attacking. When the Romans would go to war, they would take these shields in the front lines of the battle and would stand side by side with one another and formed a line that could extend as long as a mile or longer. They would have archers who stood behind this wall and shot as they progressed forward and provided a great barricade to hide behind when going against the swords and spears of the enemy. Often when advancing against an enemy they would form what is called the testudo, or tortoise formation. This was when the Roman soldiers would form a tight formation and tight square, those in front laid shields in front of them. The men in the middle on the outside would hold them to their side while the others would hold them over their heads and those in back turned facing the enemy in formation so that they were covered on all sides from the arrows of the enemy. This would allow the Romans to be able to lay siege against enemies without fear of arrows and falling rocks hurting them.

The type of shield that Paul tells these Christians that they are to take up is the shield of **faith.** The word that Paul uses for faith is (πίστις) Pistis which means "to be fully persuaded, convinced, have full confidence in, to trust in." The writer of Hebrews defines faith in (Hebrews 11:1) "Now faith is the assurance of things hoped for, the conviction of things not seen." Faith in the Bible is not some blind leap into the dark hoping that something is out there but not having any knowledge of that which they claim to believe in. However, when you look in the scriptures you can see that faith is based on that which you know of God, based upon the revealed knowledge of God in creation and the Scriptures to believe in. True Biblical faith consists in at least two essential ways and that being the ascent of the mind and the ascent of the will. As one looks unto the Scriptures and gains a knowledge of God, they must be fully persuaded and convinced in their mind the truth of God as given in the Bible. The other aspect of faith is the ascent of the will, which entails putting one's full trust in God and the truths they find of him in the Scriptures. When one fully trust God they place their full confidence in truths of God as found in the Scriptures and then put into application the truths into their lives, to conform them into the image of Christ. Biblical faith is having the assurance of the promises and truths of God and having the confidence and trust in them in our daily lives. Faith is the means by which we attain heavenly realities and make them realities into our own lives.

The reason these Christians needed to have their shield of faith was that they might be able to **you will be able to extinguish all the flaming arrows.** In ancient Rome when enemies went into battle against Rome one of the tactics that the enemies would use to try to attack Rome was shoot arrows at them. These arrows were covered on the ends with cloth and then usually dipped in pitch or tar and they became **flaming arrows.** These arrows were also known to be dipped in the blood of poisonous vipers so that it would cause not only external burning but also internal burning from the poison if they were shot. These flaming arrows also were designed to cause panic to the soldier even if they arrow never hit a soldier. These flaming arrows could hit the shield Roman soldier and setting the shield on fire. This was to cause fear in the soldier that he might throw his shield aside and making him very vulnerable to attack. They would shoot their arrows rapidly so as to cause great confusion and chaos to cause soldiers to get out of formation or to panic. The flaming arrows were lethal even if it missed it's intended target for often, they would set ablaze objects around it. FF Bruce said "Even when such a missile was caught by the shield and did not penetrate to the body, say Livy (Roman Historian), it caused panic, because it was thrown when well alight and its motion through the air made it blaze most fiercely, so that the soldier was tempted to get rid of his burning shield and expose himself to the enemy's spear-thrusts. But the shield of faith not only catches the incendiary devices but extinguishes them."[45]

The importance of the shield for the Roman soldier was that they would **be able to extinguish** the flaming arrows that were shot at them. The word for **extinguish** here is (σβέννυμι) Sbennumi which means "put out or quench." The shield gave the soldier the ability to be able to withstand the fiery arrows of the enemy by putting them out. Roman soldiers would soak their shields in water so that the leather on the shield was soaked in water. This was done so that when they went into battle the flaming arrows would hit the water with leather and it would cause the fire to be put out. The Roman soldier would take extra care of their shield to keep it in good condition for battle. Every morning the soldier would take out his shield and he would put oil on it and rub it on the shield to keep in good condition as to not dry or crack, and that would remain firm and stable. The arrows that these Christians needed a shield for against their enemy **the evil one.** The Greek word for evil one is (πονηρός) Poneras that means "wicked, evil, bad, malicious" If Paul was talking about here of a physical enemy he would have said against the barbarians or the Greeks, but he is talking about a spiritual one. The reason as to why he is called the evil one because that describes his character and his nature to do bad and promote wickedness. This word for evil one is used 10 times in the New Testament. Each time that they are used it is always used in reference to Satan such as in (John 17:15) "I do not ask You to take them out of the world, but to keep them from the evil one." We see it again in (2 Thessalonians 3:3) "But the Lord is faithful, and He will strengthen and protect you from the evil one." The evil one will try to shoot many flaming arrows at the Christians which include things such as temptations, accusations, lies, guilt, shame, hate, bitterness, greed, immorality, and many other fiery arrows. It is for this reason Paul tells these Christians they needed to be shielded by faith so

---

[45] Precept Austin. (May 24, 2018). *Ephesians 6:16-17 Commentary.* Retrieved from https://www.preceptaustin.org/ephesians_616-17

that when the devil shot his flaming arrows, they would be able to put them out by their faith.

It is important to notice that Paul does not say some of the flaming arrows but rather he says all the flaming arrows will be put out thru Christ power. It does not matter what arrows that the enemy will shoot to set the Christians aflame they can all be extinguished by faith. Physical arrows that enemies of Rome would have shot have many related elements to how the Devil shoots his fiery arrows at the Christian. For instance, an arrow when it is shot is quick upon the release and could penetrate a person before they knew what happened to them. In a similar manner, Satan shoots his flaming missiles at us that are quick often don't know what is happening to us. As an example, one can wake up in the morning one day and then all of a sudden you just feel hit with anger, depression, or anxious for no reason. If a person does not recognize these fiery arrows as coming from the Devil and don't resist them by faith, they begin to own those feelings and emotions. As result they let them linger upon them from the rest of the day and instead of quenching them by faith, they set the individuals emotions aflame. When the devil shoots these arrows the one must put up the shield and say in mind or thought or out loud the word of God that you have faith in which says (Psalm 42:11) "Why are you in despair, O my soul? And why have you become disturbed within me? Hope in God, for I shall yet praise Him, the help of my countenance and my God." In those moments your faith says I am not going to dwell upon these unwanted thoughts and not let them control me today, I by faith believe you God will help me decipher out why do I feel this way for and put these emotions and thoughts in the proper order in my life.

Another aspect about the arrow is that they are penetrating that can be lethal and destructive. In a similar manner when the devil shoots his flaming arrows, they are penetrating that are lethal and destructive to an individual. Sometimes the devil will send arrows that will penetrate our very heart in the form of temptations to appeal to our desires so that he appeals to our lusts, addictions, wealth, sports, or material goods to penetrate your heart to gain access into it that he might take control. When he shoots that arrow at you put up the shield and say in mind or thought or out loud the word of God that you have faith in which says (1 Corinthians 6:9-10) "Or do you not know that the unrighteous will not inherit the kingdom of God? Do not be deceived; neither fornicators, nor idolaters, nor adulterers, nor effeminate, nor homosexuals, nor thieves, nor the covetous, nor drunkards, nor revilers, nor swindlers, will inherit the kingdom of God." In so you are saying I believe God that you see me in these moments and that I will be held accountable for every work that I do and by faith I will refuse this devilish offer. Faith will say in those moments that I know the devil pleasures are empty delights, that he offers satisfaction but yet delivers destruction, and by faith, I will refuse this devilish delight. Charles Hodge wrote that "He showers arrows of fire on the soul of the believer; who, if unprotected by the shield of faith, would soon perish. It is a common experience of the people of God that at times horrible thoughts, blasphemous, skeptical, malignant, crowd upon the mind, which cannot be accounted for on any ordinary law of mental action, and which cannot be dislodged. They stick like burning arrows, and fill the soul with agony. They can be quenched only by faith; by calling on Christ for help. These, however, are not the only kind of fiery darts; nor are they most dangerous. There are others which enkindle passion, inflame ambition, excite cupidity, pride, discontent, or vanity; producing a flame which our deceitful heart is not so prompt to extinguish, and which often allowed to burn until it produces great injury even destruction. Against these most dangerous weapons of the evil one, the only protection is faith."[46]

At times the devil will shoot his penetrating arrows of doubt that he will cause you to think twice about that Bible you are reading, the reasons why you are going to church or wasting your money giving it to the church so that you just stop doing all these things. Whether things on TV or a false teacher or it may just be a thought that would come through the mind. He sends this arrow to penetrate your mind and heart as to cause confusion, doubt, deceit, and fear to lead you astray. When he shoots that arrow at you put up the shield and say in mind or thought or out loud the word of God that you have faith in which says (2 Timothy 3:16-17) "All Scripture is inspired by God and profitable for teaching, for reproof, for correction, for training in righteousness; so that the man of God may be adequate, equipped for every good work." Or passages like (2 Peter 1:20-21) "But know this first of all, that no prophecy of Scripture is a matter of one's own interpretation, for no prophecy was ever made by an act of human will, but men moved by the Holy Spirit spoke from God." Your faith says I may not have all the answers to all the Bible questions or to all that happens in the Bible or how it happened but I do trust that they are true and I believe that as your word says you inspired men to write it and because of the impact made on my life I believe it.

Another aspect in regard to arrows is that they are deadly and designed to kill and to wound that in which they come in contact with. In a similar manner when the Devil shoots his arrows at us, he does so as a means to kill and wound the Christian. This is the very nature of who Satan is in accordance with what Jesus said in (John 10:10) "The thief comes only to steal and kill and destroy; I came that they may have life and have it abundantly." One of the ways in which the devil does this is to shoot

---

[46] Charles Hodge (1994) *Commentary on the Epistle to the Ephesians.* Grand Rapids: Wm B. Eerdmans, pp. 386-387

arrows to flame insecurities inside of the individual so that they will focus on their externals such as how ugly you look, how untalented you are, how worthless you really are, and how stupid you look or you would look so don't try it. He will shoot his arrows to inflame your insecurities, inferiorities, lusts, jealousies and many other areas as a means to kill and wound the Christians soldier. Other times he shoots his arrows to inflame us with worthlessness and hopelessness as if there is no purpose to your existence so that you will hate yourself and life. In those moments one by faith must remember what the Scripture says thru David in (Psalm 139:16-19) "For You formed my inward parts; you wove me in my mother's womb. I will give thanks to you, for I am fearfully and wonderfully made; wonderful are Your works, and my soul knows it very well. My frame was not hidden from you when I was made in secret, and skillfully wrought in the depths of the earth; your eyes have seen my unformed substance; and in Your book were all written the days that were ordained *for me*, when as yet there was not one of them." It will be one's faith in these truths that when the Devil seeks to kill the Christian with these deadly arrows.

EPHESIANS 6:17

By Brent Calloway

Ephesians 6:17 Updated American Standard Version (UASV)

[17] And take the helmet of salvation, and the sword of the Spirit, which is the word of God.

Paul now moves onto the fifth piece of armor that is essential for the Christian soldier. **The helmet** in which Paul is referring to here is the (περικεφαλαία) Perikephalaia. It was called by the Romans as the Galea and it covered the head of the soldier to protect him from any blow that may come to his head. This was the last piece of the armor that the soldier would usually put on and maybe the most essential in many ways because even if all his other parts were on his body and yet his helmet was on it would leave him extremely vulnerable and susceptible to a quick death if not greatly crippled or paralyzed. If a Roman soldier didn't have the helmet on then it would be no point to have the rest of armor would be of very little use and quite meaningless, because on blow to the head would render the belt, breastplate, shoes, and shield useless and therefore was essential for the Roman soldier to wear. Of all the pieces of the armor that Paul mentions the helmet is given the shortest description but nevertheless it is one of the most valuable.

The common Roman soldiers' helmet was made of metal typically of bronze or iron, however, a poor soldier would often times have helmets made of leather that were bound with metal for protection. The helmets were not mass produced but rather they were made and created individually. The helmet was an essential part of the armor for the soldier as it protected the face and the cheek area, along with covering the forehead and protecting the back of the neck. It protected the soldier's head and the only thing that was left exposed to the soldier was the eyes, nose, and mouth. So strong were these helmets it was said that the only thing in which could actually penetrate them was hammers and axes. They would have protected them from arrows coming their way, daggers and the sword that would have been used by their opponents against them. For some soldier, their helmet was lined on the inside with a sponge or felt for the sake of comfort reasons. Some helmet was adorned with a horsehair crest for looks as to distinguish the rank of military officers when they went to battle.

James Boice said of the Roman helmet "The helmet had a band to protect the forehead and plates for the cheeks and extended down in back to protect the neck. When the helmet was strapped in place, it exposed little besides the eyes, nose, and mouth. The metal helmets, due to their weight, were lined with a sponge or felt. Virtually the only weapons which could penetrate a metal helmet were hammer or axes."[47] The helmet for the Roman soldier not only gave him protection in the fight but it also provided for him, the confidence in the fight. Now the helmet was used more for protection against more close hand to hand combat and give him the confidence to fight. This was not just the confidence to fight hand and hand so that it would not get stabbed by a sword but also it was protection against any flying javelins or against any flaming arrows that would be coming their way to hit them in the head. If the soldier didn't have the confidence to be able to fight, he would either be too full of anxiety to fight, causing him to fight timidly, or he would not fight at all. He might even have thought he would die quickly. In the same manner, the Christian is to wear their spiritual helmet to protect their mind.

The mind needs to be protected because when it is one of the most vital and vulnerable parts that the devil will try to strike at and as result has destroyed and wounded and killed many by making major blows to their mind. For it is true that we will act the way that we think and that is why the scriptures define that the mind is a battlefield that is always being warred against by the devil to take control and as means to gain access into our lives as to dominate us. If the devil can manipulate as to affect and sway the mind, he will then control our actions. Paul described the warfare against the mind in (Romans 7:18-23) "For I know that nothing good dwells in me, that is, in my flesh; for the willing is present in me, but the doing of the good is not. For the good that I want, I do not do, but I practice the very evil that I do not want. But if I am doing the very thing I do not want, I am no longer the one doing it, but sin which dwells in me. I find then the principle that evil is present in me, the one who wants to do good. For I joyfully concur with the law of God in the inner man, but I see a different law in the members of my body, waging war against the law of my mind and making me a prisoner of the law of sin which is in my members." Paul would say again in (Romans 8:5-8) "For those who are according to the flesh set their minds on the things of the flesh, but those who according to the Spirit, the things of the Spirit. For the mind set on the flesh is death, but the mind set on the Spirit is life and peace, because the mind set on the flesh is hostile toward God; for it does not subject itself to the law of God, for it is not even able to do so, and those who are in the flesh cannot please God."

The helmet the Christian is to put on Paul says is salvation which is the Greek word σωτήριος (Soterios) which means "to rescue, deliver, save." Yet

---

[47] Steve Ramsey. (March 11, 2018). *The Helmet of Salvation and Sword of the Spirit.* Retrieved from http://www.moleopedia.com/the-helmet-of-salvation-and-the-sword-of-the-spirit/

what specifically does salvation mean? First, when we are saved that entails that we are saved of sin as past event. This means that when you repented from sin that you were saved from the sins that God held in judgment over you. So, salvation entails being saved from the sin that you once lived in and now given a new life to live with the past being forgiven. That is seen from the scriptures in looking at verses like (Acts 10:43) "…everyone who believes in Him receives forgiveness of sins." It is for this reason that Paul in considering his past and knowing his sin and past life was forgiven would write in (Philippians 3:13-14) "…forgetting what lies behind and reaching forward to what lies ahead, I press on toward the goal for the prize of the upward call of God in Christ Jesus." When we come to Christ to repent of our sins and confess him to be Lord then we have been saved the sin that once held judgment of God over us instead has been exchanged for a hand of grace and mercy in which we can now be a friend and child of God. The judgment of our sin and the debt we owed was paid at the cross and the moment we confess and believe then our debt has been paid and the judgment of God against us has been laid down.

The second aspect of salvation is that we not only been saved from sins of the past but saved from the current power of sin. This means that the power of sin that once dominated us our hearts, minds, thoughts, desires, attitudes, actions, etc. has now been broken so that it no longer has keeps us in bondage, but we have been freed from its power. This is not to say that it does not still affect us but rather it no longer now controls and dominates us. So that we have by the power of Christ in us the ability to be able to overcome sin that once in our own nature was impossible to do and can by the power of Christ living in you and ability to be able to overcome sin as seen in (Titus 2:11-14) "For the grace of God has appeared, bringing salvation to all men, instructing us to deny ungodliness and worldly desires and to live sensibly, righteously and godly in the present age, looking for the blessed hope and appearing of the glory of our great God and Savior, Christ Jesus, who gave Himself for us to redeem us from every lawless deed, and to purify for Himself a people from His own possession, zealous for good deeds." Consider also what Paul wrote as well when he said in (Romans 6:17-18) "But thanks be to God that though you were slaves of sin, you became obedient from the heart to that form of teaching to which you were committed, and having been freed from sin, you became slaves of righteousness." A final aspect of salvation is that not only are saved from the guilt of past sin, and the power of current sin, but we also look forward to eternity where one day we will be without sin. This provided that we have not only repented of sin but that we daily continue to repent and strive to live a holy life in obedience to God's command and serve Him and then as result we will one day in eternity with God be without sin. – 1 Corinthians 15:42-44; 48-49.

How exactly though does salvation function like a helmet to protect the mind? Paul answers that question when he said in (1 Thessalonians 5:8-10) "But since we are of the day, let us be sober, having put on the breastplate of faith and love, and as a helmet, the hope of salvation. For God has not destined us for wrath, but for obtaining salvation through our Lord Jesus Christ, who died for us, so that whether we are awake or asleep, we will live together with Him." When you look at this text what we can see that Paul refers to the helmet as the hope of salvation. Therefore, the helmet of salvation is important for the Christian because it offers them hope. The Greek word for hope is ἐλπίς (Elpis) "trust, confidence, expectation" or in other words a confident expectation that something is true will happen to place trust in. For Roman soldier one of the greatest aspects about the helmet that they wore was that it gave them the confidence to be able to fight without worrying about arrows, swords, or daggers, then they could win the battle and gain the victory. The helmet of salvation, therefore, is important for the Christian soldier because it protects him by giving him confidence in the midst of the war. Yet in what ways does salvation give the Christian confidence exactly?

First salvation gives the Christian confidence in regard to their past. One of the greatest attacks of the Devil upon the mind is to produce thoughts that will destroy their confidence in Christ. The Devil loves to deceive people into thinking that they can't be saved in the first place because they have been too sinful, and that lie keeps many from coming to Christ. Yet even if he can't stop a person from coming to Christ, he then will seek to lie to Christians after they do sin perhaps, they are not a Christian for why would they have done what they just did. These lies are intended to destroy the confidence that Christians have as a means to stifle their relationship with God and often time leaves them maimed or crippled in their walk with God. It is for this reason that having confidence in the work of Christ upon the cross gives the Christian soldier protection around his mind. When you have this confidence, you don't have to walk around feeling as if God hates or is angry at you, holding your sin over you as if you can never be forgiven of your sins. To believe this creates depression and anxiety, and stress upon the soul that affects you mentally, emotionally, physically, and spiritually and hinders your walk with Christ. Yet to have the hope your sins have been forgiven gives you the confidence that God indeed does love you and accepts you and wants to be in relationship with you, and longs to see you in heaven as much as you would want to see him. You see rejection is the worst destroyer of hope, because when you believed that you are not loved you feel you have no worth or value and no reason to live, but to have the hope that you are loved and have value and told that then it makes you want to live and continue no matter what happens.. When you know that God loves you and the rest of the world hates you it doesn't matter that love alone triumphs all the hate in the world. This is extremely important to have confidence in knowing your forgiven and loved because of the fact that the devil will try to persuade your mind and speak lies to it that you are not.

That is why for the Christian he will use that to keep you from Christ but if saved use to try to paralyze your walk with God, so as to get you to doubt that God could really love you after you committed that certain sin of the past. One of the greatest lies and deceptions that he will use to depress your soul and weigh it down to make it seem impossible to please God that he is not pleased with you is to make you think past sins can't be forgiven and as result throw armor down and give up. It will be those times that your confidence in being saved and based off God's word will come to protect your mind in understanding that the Bible says (Micah 7:18-19) "Who is a God like you, who pardons iniquity and passes over the rebellious act of the remnant of His possession? He does not retain His anger forever, because He delights in unchanging love. He will again have compassion on us; He will tread our iniquities under foot. Yes, you will cast all their sins into the depths of the sea." Or like what Isaiah wrote of God in (Isaiah 1:18) "Come now, and let us reason together, says the Lord, though your sins are as scarlet, they will be as white as snow; though they are red like crimson, they will be like wool."

Another way that salvation gives confidence to the Christian is for the present here and now. As long as we live in the flesh, we will still have a sin nature about us until we receive our glorified bodies in Heaven. Until that time no Christian will ever live the perfect life, they will still fall into sin. Although it should no longer be a habitual pattern of their life, they will still sin. Yet many times the Devil will take those moments of sin as a means to capitalize on trying to destroy the confidence of the Christian as to how God could love them, especially the times when they sin. It will be in those times that the Christian can find confidence in what Jesus said in (John 6:37-39) "All that the Father gives Me will come to Me, and the one who comes to Me I will certainly not cast out. For I have come down from heaven, not to do My own will, but the will of Him who sent Me. This is the will of Him who sent Me, that of all that He has given Me I lose nothing but raise it up on the last day." Again when the Devil attacks the mind with doubt of God's love towards them even after repentance of their sin they can find confidence in what Jesus said in (John 10:27-30) "My sheep hear My voice, and I know them, and they follow Me; and I give eternal life to them, and they will never perish; and no one will snatch them out of My hand. My Father, who has given *them* to Me, is greater than all; and no one is able to snatch *them* out of the Father's hand. I and the Father are one." When Christians have been saved thru the blood of Christ that gives them the confidence to be able to fight and stand firm. Knowing that one is saved is one of the greatest things to know, namely, that they can be forgiven of sin currently when they repent and that one day sin will be taken away if they continue to abide in Christ. Hope for the Christian is an anchor for the soul against devil's thunder, and storms of life's circumstances to continue to remain standing and endure as the writer of Hebrews would say in (Hebrews 6:19) "...we have as an anchor of the soul, a hope both sure and steadfast..." Without hope or the expectation of the goodness of God or eternal life, this would be nothing more than just an existence to survive in, but with hope then life becomes vibrant and meaningful.

Finally, salvation not only gives confidence from the past, in the present but also for the future as well for the Christian. It can be difficult at times when we are bombarded with constant news of children getting raped, school getting shot up, politicians fighting, tornadoes destroying, and constant wars. All of this can weigh you down and get you wore out and almost seem that there is no God that indeed even exists at all, so as to make you give up on hope and faith. The Devil can use these things to make a Christian speculate the reality of God and mercy of God that such events take place. For many, he has deceived them well enough to leave the faith or to be hardened towards God in the midst of such things. In these times the Christian needs to have confidence in the fact that one day the Bible says this will indeed be done away with and this will be no more and you have that to look forward to as bad as it gets now this will not last forever, but we battle in this sinful world now for temporal amount of time but eventually will have an eternity where none of this will ever bother or be again. We can have this confidence from the scriptures as seen in (Revelation 22:14-15) "Blessed are those who wash their robes, so that they may have the right to the tree of life and may enter by the gates into the city. Outside are the dogs and the sorcerers and the immoral persons and the murderers and the idolaters, and everyone who loves and practices lying." This truth can give confidence to the Christian and hope for the future when Christ establishes the new heavens and the new earth.

and the sword of the Spirit, which is the word of God.

The seventh piece of the armor that Paul mentions for these Christians is **the sword of the spirit.** Of all the pieces for the armor that Paul gave to the Christians to do battle with up to this point, they have been for defensive purposes. The sword is the only piece of the armor that for the Roman served as an offensive weapon. The Roman soldier would carry on his left side a dagger in which was about 6-11 inches long called a Pugio. This dagger was used when all else failed and his sword didn't work then he could pull out this dagger and make quick stabs and jabs to the enemy. This was typically used for up close hand to hand combat. This dagger was designed not designed so much to kill but rather to severely injure the enemy. A Roman soldier would also carry with them into battle a spear called a pilum, and many times would carry two of them. A pilum was over 6 feet long and made of wood and a long piece of iron at the front with a sharp heavy point of iron. These spears could be thrown up at distance of 100 ft. but they were most effective around 50-65 feet. The Romans would throw these spears at their enemies to intimidate and cause them to panic. The spear weighed about 10 pounds and when it was thrown it could stick into the enemy's shield. This would give the Romans advantage for if it stuck in the enemies shield it would bend so that they could not pull it out. With the spear stuck into the shield, it would add extra weight on the shield and the Romans hoped for the enemies to throw down their shields to make them easier targets. The Romans were known to throw these Pilum's while a considerable distance out, before engaging in an attack.

The kind of sword that Paul is referring to here is not the Roman pugio or pilum, but rather he is referring to the sword, known in the Latin as Gladius. The Greek word for **sword** that Paul uses here is Machaira which refers to a small sword. This sword was a short 18-inch sword that was sharp on both sides and lightweight that made it easy to maneuver. The sword was used for short and quick stabs that were lethal in hand to hand combat and small enough so that the soldier could swing it easily. The Roman formation consisted of three rows of legionaries each with about three feet (or one meter) of space per man. Each row was separated by about six feet (or two meters). When closing with the enemy the heavy spears would be launched to break down the opposing formation. The gladius was then drawn, and the enemy would be engaged by the short sword. The sword could also be employed with a hacking motion going as far as hacking off limbs and striking the torso of the enemy. Soldiers were even trained to slice at an opponent's legs beneath his shield if this offered the only opening.

Paul describes here the sword that the Christians are to fight with, which is not a physical sword but a spiritual sword, and in particular the **sword of the spirit.** Paul refers to the Christians sword of that of the spirit because the sword that he referring to is the word of God. Paul calls it the sword of the spirit because the inspiration behind the word of God when it was penned by men was the Holy Spirit as they were moved along to write under the divine inspiration that God gave them to do so. Paul spoke of this when he said in (2 Timothy 3:16-17) "All Scripture is inspired by God and profitable for teaching, for reproof, for correction, for training in righteousness; so that the man of God may be adequate, equipped for every good work." When the Scripture writers wrote God didn't change their nature or thinking abilities but rather worked through their own personality, writing styles and abilities as they wrote as God inspired them to do. So that the words they were writing was the very words of God Himself as given to them as expressed in their writings by the Holy Spirit. Peter spoke of this when he said in (2 Peter 1:20-21) "But know this first of all, that no prophecy of Scripture is a matter of one's own interpretation, for no prophecy was ever made by an act of human will, but men moved by the Holy Spirit spoke from God." Therefore, the Word of God is the writings of men of God who were inspired of God in the power of the Spirit of God to write the very words of God in human form and expressions that man may know God.

Paul goes onto explain that the sword that Paul is talking about is the **word of God.** The writers of Hebrews wrote in (Hebrews 4:12) "For the word of God is living and active and sharper than any two-edged sword and piercing as far as the division of soul and spirit, of both joints and marrow, and able to judge the thoughts and intentions of the heart." The word of God is the greatest offensive weapon that the Christians has to kill the devil's attacks. The word of God like a sword cuts down the devils lies, slices through his deceptions, and penetrates through all of his manipulations and intimidations. It is worth noting that the word that Paul uses here for word of God is the Greek word ῥῆμα (Rhema) and it denotes "a spoken word." A Rhema word is not just word spoken in general, rather they are specific words that pertain to or are needful in a specific moment or situation at hand. The greatest example we have a Rhema word used against the Devil is found in Christ as he was tempted by Satan in Matthew 4:1-11.

The devil comes to Jesus with his first lie in which he said to Jesus (Matthew 4:3) "If You are the Son of God, command that these stones become bread." The devil was tempting Jesus to use his own power to satisfy his own needs apart from God to satisfy his own flesh. In other words, he was tempting Jesus to be the god of his own life instead of trusting God give him all that he would need for life. He wanted to instill doubt into the mind of Christ in regard to the trustworthiness of his position with God as his son. After all of God was really his Father, why would be out in the desert without any food or water. Jesus cuts through this lie, not by coming at the devil with his own words, but rather he gives the Devil a Rhema word when he said in Matthew 4:4 "It is written, 'MAN SHALL NOT LIVE ON BREAD ALONE, BUT ON EVERY WORD THAT PROCEEDS OUT OF THE MOUTH OF GOD." Jesus here quotes directly from the word of God by quoting an Old Testament passage found in Deuteronomy 8:3. Jesus gave the Devil a specific and direct word from God, that cut through his lies. There will be times when the Devil and his demons will come at you to tempt you in your most vulnerable situations in similar ways. They will seek to get you to forget that God can help you through or supply you with what you need and instead tempt you to satisfy yourself by your own means in your own power without relying on God. He will come hard at you those days when you are feeling down and sad, depressed and worthless to cave into his temptations because God can't help so he tries to provide an alternative to fix the problem in his own way. It will be in those moments you need a Rhema word to help you to know that God alone satisfies such as (Matthew 5:6) "Blessed are those who hunger and thirst for righteousness, for they shall be satisfied." Or as Jesus said in (John 6:35) "I am the bread of life; he who comes to Me will not hunger, and he who believes in Me will never thirst." When the Christian has those scripture memorized and quotes them when the devil seeks to tempt them to compromise or find satisfaction in other ways, it will slice through his lies and make him flee.

Again we see the devil come at Jesus a second time with another deception as he took him to the pinnacle of the temple and said in Matthew 4:5-6 "If You are the Son of God, throw Yourself down; for it is written, 'HE WILL COMMAND HIS ANGELS CONCERNING YOU'; and 'ON *their* HANDS THEY WILL BEAR YOU UP, SO THAT YOU WILL NOT STRIKE YOUR FOOT AGAINST A STONE.'" Here the devil was appealing to the pride of Jesus in getting Jesus to bypass the cross and just jump down and allow God to do a miracle. This way the crowd would be amazed and this incredible miracle and would come and follow him, instead of having to follow through with a bloody cross. The Devil wanted Jesus to test God's hand to see if he really would save him and was seeking to instigate Jesus to try to prove God for his own advantage. Yet Jesus stands his ground and again uses a Rhema word of God to slice through the devil's deception when he said in Matthew 4:7 "On the other hand, it is written, 'YOU SHALL NOT PUT THE LORD YOUR GOD TO THE TEST." Once again Jesus speaks from the Old Testament when he quotes here Deuteronomy 6:16. Again Jesus uses a specific verse to cut open the Devil's lies. Then the Devil tries a third attempt to seek to manipulate Christ when it says in Matthew 4:8-9 " Again, the devil took Him to a very high mountain and showed Him all the kingdoms of the world and their glory; and he said to Him, "All these things I will give You, if You fall down and worship me." Here the devil sought to manipulate Jesus into compromise by seeking to trade his Heavenly glory for earthly glory. Once again, a ploy by the Devil to keep Jesus from his death on the cross and the resurrection, which was a certain defeat for the Devil. Yet again Jesus penetrates this manipulation by using a Rhema word from God in saying in (Matthew 4:10) "Go, Satan! For it is written, 'YOU SHALL WORSHIP THE LORD YOUR GOD, AND SERVE HIM ONLY." Jesus displayed the killing power the word of God has against the devil when it is used against him in warfare. The result of Jesus quoting the word of God to the Devil is found in Matthew 4:11 "Then the devil left Him; and behold, angels came and *began* to minister to Him." There will be other times when the Devil and his demons will attack us through our pride, by either getting us to believe we too good we don't need God or that things going so well we don't need to lean upon him, or thinking that we can control our lives by making our own decisions or cutting our own paths apart from him, without seeing the dangers therein. It will be in those times you will need a Rhema word such as in (Proverbs 11:2) "When pride comes, then comes disgrace, but with humility comes wisdom" or (Proverbs 16:18) "Pride goes before destruction, a haughty spirit before a fall." It will be as the Christian has these truths memorized and uses them against the Devil that it will cut through his lies and he will flee.

We see the Devil come at Jesus again for a third time to tempt him in by taking him to a mountain showing him all the kingdoms of the world and their glory. The Devil then said to Jesus in (Matthew 4:9) "All these things I will give You if You fall down and worship me." In showing Jesus all the kingdoms of the world, he is showing Jesus all the riches, power, authority, and control that he can have. It was an effort on the part of the Devil to seek to influence to bypass the cross the pain and agony of what it would cost him to do so. Rather just bow down to him and that would be all that would need to be to gain the authority over the world, that only cross could bring. He wanted Jesus to compromise so that he could gain control. Yet again Jesus responds not by some general summary of the Bible but gives a specific statement or Rhema word when he said in (Matthew 4:10) "'Go, Satan! For it is written, 'You shall worship the Lord your God, and serve Him only.'" Jesus here is quoting from specifically from

(Deuteronomy 6:13) "You shall fear only the Lord your God, and you shall worship Him." and (Deuteronomy 10:20) "You shall fear the Lord your God; you shall serve Him..." Here Jesus uses this specific statement against the devil as a means to say that only one worthy to be worshiped. There will no doubt be times as well when the devil will come at you to try to appeal to your heart and mind to compromise or make compromises so that you can get what you want quickly without waiting on God. He tempts the Christian to compromise with addictions It will be in those times that you will need a Rhema word to help you through such as in (1 John 2:15-17) "Do not love the world nor the things in the world. If anyone loves the world, the love of the Father is not in him. For all that is in the world, the lust of the flesh, and the lust of the eyes and the boastful pride of life is not from the Father but is from the world. The world is passing away, and also its lusts; but the one who does the will of God lives forever."

After Jesus had spoken the Rhema word against Satan Matthew then records in (Matthew 4:11) "Then the devil left Him; and behold, angels came and *began* to minister to Him." It is interesting that this is the first time we have in the scriptures that it is recorded that the devil actually leaves and flees, and it is due to the fact that Jesus spoke the word of God unto him. As Christians, we must be equipped with the word of God, for it is our only part of the offense against Devil in a spiritual war. Yet as we have seen through the example of Jesus that the Christian can take confidence in the fact that the devil can't stand up to the weapon of God's word. He will, and he must flee, it does mean that he will stop attacking but the word of God reverses the attack on Satan. Paul also would use the word of God in his war against Satan when he said to the church in Corinth in (2 Corinthians 10:3-6) "For though we walk in the flesh, we do not war according to the flesh, for the weapons of our warfare are not of the flesh, but divinely powerful for the destruction of fortresses. *We are* destroying speculations and every lofty thing raised up against the knowledge of God, and *we are* taking every thought captive to the obedience of Christ, **and** we are ready to punish all disobedience, whenever your obedience is complete." It is essential for the Christians to be equipped with the word of God in their knowledge and memorization of it, ready to use it to counter any attack the devil brings whether it be lies, deceit, manipulations, or any other form of attack. John MacArthur said, the "Christian who does not know God's Word well cannot use it well. Satan will invariably find out where we are ignorant or confused and attack us there. Scripture is not a broadsword to be waved indiscriminately, but a dagger to be used with great precision."[48]

---

[48] MacArthur, John (1986). *The MacArthur New Testament Commentary: Ephesians.* Chicago: Moody Press, pg. 370

EPHESIANS 6:18

By Brent Calloway

Ephesians 6:18 Updated American Standard Version (UASV)

¹⁸ Through all prayer and petition praying at all times in the Spirit, and with this in view, keep awake with all perseverance and making supplication for all the holy ones.

Paul adds one more piece to the Christian armor for battle and that is he tells these Christians and that is as they put on the armor of God they were to do so **with all prayer.** It is important to take note of the fact that uses the word **with** here in regard to prayer. This serves as a connective word to connect what Paul has just said with what he is about to say now in regard to prayer. Paul is saying to these Christians, along with putting on the seven pieces of the armor, are to do so **with all prayer.** It is interesting to note that when it comes to our weapon of prayer that Paul has no comparison by which to make with a Roman soldier's armor. This is because only those who are in soldiers of Christ in God's army have this powerful weapon accessible to them. When it comes to prayer there is nothing to compare it with because this only something that God could create and give power to. Perhaps the greatest weapon the Christians has in their war against Devil and his demons is prayer.

Thru prayer these Christians would have the strength and stamina to wear their armor and fight the spiritual war daily. All of the pieces of the armor need to be in place in order to fight in the spiritual war, but the means by which these Christian would activate those pieces of armor through the source of prayer. Prayer is the generating force that gives power to the armor that ignites, motivates, and initiates the desire to want to put the armor on and to keep it on. So important in prayer in the spiritual battle that without it you will not be able to fight and will become a casualty of war. It is also important to emphasize the fact Paul says they were to pray with **at all times.** The Greek word that is used here for times is the word καιρός (Kairos) and it refers to a point and time that is specific and precise. It refers not so much to a succession of minutes to hours but rather specific periods of opportunity when they arise whenever they come and whenever the devil attacks. Paul is saying that at any and all times when the Devil springs his attack the Christian to be ready to fight with his armor on and prayer.

Paul not only tells these Christian the necessity of prayer in spiritual warfare, but he tells them how to pray in times of spiritual war. Paul says that they were to pray and that is by way of **petition.** The Greek word for petition used here is (δέησις) Deesis meaning "to beg, plead, to want." This word carries with it the idea that it is not so much a general prayer being prayed but rather is a specific prayer that is made in regard to specific needs, situations and is a matter of urgency to the one making the request. These Christians would be in some intense spiritual warfare and they would be times that they would have to make specific petitions unto God. There would be other times that they would have to petition before the Lord in moments of desperation to help in critical moments. When it seems like the devil is overwhelming one with his lies and his seductions, and facing intense warfare, they would need to be able to petition God.

Then Paul the manner in which they were to pray and that was **in the Spirit.** Paul has elsewhere written of the importance of praying in the Spirit when he wrote in (Jude 20) "But you, beloved, building yourselves up on your most holy faith, praying in the Holy Spirit..." Paul again would write in reference to this in (Romans 8:28) " In the same way the Spirit also helps our weakness; for we do not know how to pray as we should, but the Spirit Himself intercedes for *us* with groanings too deep for words; and He who searches the hearts knows what the mind of the Spirit is, because He intercedes for the saints according to *the will of* God." Finally, Paul would also speak of this when he wrote in (1 Corinthians 14:13-15) "Therefore let one who speaks in a tongue pray that he may interpret. For if I pray in a tongue, my spirit prays, but my mind is unfruitful. What is *the outcome* then? I will pray with the spirit and I will pray with the mind also; I will sing with the spirit and I will sing with the mind also." When Paul writes about praying in the Spirit here, he is not so much about the words that they were saying but rather the manner in which they were praying. It is the type of prayer that prays as the Spirit of God directs and leads the prayer, under the Spirit's influence. To pray with the Spirit is a prayer of urgency in which total dependence and trust is laid upon God for direction and guidance under the Spirit's control to pray in the Holy Spirit entails that there is a deep longing and seeking of God for his direction, help, and protection in the midst of a certain spiritual attack that you are facing. So that we are no praying some half-hearted fake prayers that go no farther than our own four walls. John Bunyan said in regard to prayer "Pray often, for prayer is a shield to the soul, a sacrifice to God, and a scourge for Satan."[49] Paul continues his thoughts on prayer by telling these Christians that as they are to **be on the alert.** The Greek word here is ἀγρυπνέω (Agrupneo) and it means "to go without sleep." This is in the present tense which indicates that this is to be a believer's continue lifestyle and to be one of continued vigilance and awareness of all times of the activity of the enemy and how he is coming at you to know how to handle him correctly.

---

[49] John Bunyan, (1872) *The Complete Works of John Bunyan.* Philadelphia: Bradley, Garretson & Co.; Illustrated Edition edition. pg. 80.

This is the same word that is used when Jesus would say to his disciples in the garden in of his return in the last days in (Mark 13:32-33). Though the Christian should never fear the devil, they should always be aware of him. If Christians are not in a state of continued alertness of the devil's attacks they can be easily ambushed and will suffer major losses. The devil will always attack at times that are convenient unto him and at times that the lest convenient for us. Therefore, we must continually be on the alert for he is constantly on the prowl to attack. Paul continues on and states that this prayer and alertness is to be done with **all perseverance.** The Greek word for perseverance is προσκαρτέρησις (Proskarteresis) and refers to "single steadfast course of action, that is persistent and consistent and earnest in its accomplishing of it." It is the pressing forward into doing something which one ultimately prevails in. The Christians to with pray and be alert consistently and persistently until Christ returns, or they leave this earth to go be with him. Chip Ingram said "You will probably never experience more opposition than when you pray consistently and intensely under God's Word, but they have a greater fear than Bible study. They shudder when God's people begin to pray. There are reasons that prayer doesn't always come easily for us; we have enemies who want to make it difficult. We have to break through the barriers."[50]

Finally, then Paul tells these Christians that they were not only to pray for themselves but also to pray **for all the saints.** Paul here echoes in many ways the words of Peter when he said in 1 Peter 5:8-9 "Be of sober *spirit*, be on the alert. Your adversary, the devil, prowls around like a roaring lion, seeking someone to devour. But resist him, firm in *your* faith, knowing that the same experiences of suffering are being accomplished by your brethren who are in the world." Peter makes it clear that although the Devil's attack on the Christian may many times be specifically designed to them, his attacks, in general, are leveled against all Christians universally across the world. In many ways, it is comforting to know that a Christian is not alone in his battle against the enemy but for anyone who is in Christ, they are in a war. Perhaps one of greatest deceptions of the enemy is to make a Christian feel as if he is all alone in the battle and nobody who would understand. As a result, isolation begins to take place and then it makes it easy pickings for the devil to destroy the mind and heart of a struggling Christian. However, no Christians fight alone, but every Christian across the world is in the same battle together against the Devil and his demonic cohorts. In as much as a Christian should pray for themselves during the battle, they should also be praying for their brothers and sisters around them who are going through the same battle. Warren Wiersbe

---

[50] Chip Ingram (2006). *The Invisible War.* Grand Rapids: Baker Books. Pg. 160

stated that "Prayer is the energy that enables the Christian soldier to wear the armor and to wield the sword."[51]

---

[51] Warren Wiersbe (1976) *Be Rich*. Wheaton: Victor. pg 172.

EPHESIANS 6:19

By Edward D. Andrews

Ephesians 6:19 Updated American Standard Version (UASV)

¹⁹ Pray also for me, that the words may be given to me when I open my mouth, so that I may be able to speak boldly in making known the mystery⁵² of the gospel,

that I may be able to speak boldly: Here the Greek word (*parrēsia*) rendered boldly mean **courage,** boldness, confidence, frankness (Ac 2:29; 28:31; 2 Cor. 7:4; Eph. 3:12; 1Ti 3:13; Phm 8; Heb 3:6; 4:16; 10:19, 35; 1 John 2:28; Ac 6:10) This boldness of Paul was a trait to evangelize to other to the point where it involved great risk and danger. Speaking the Word of God with boldness like Paul will be the focus of this chapter. We will be repeating this verse again for emphasis.

in making known the mystery of the gospel: Mystery; Secret: (Gr. *mystērion*) A sacred divine mystery or secret doctrine that lies with God alone, which is withheld from both the angelic body and humans, until the time he determines that it is to be revealed, and to those to whom he chooses to make it known. – Mark 4:11; Rom. 11:25; 16:25; 1 Cor. 2:1; 4:1; 13:2; 14:2; 15:51; Eph. 1:9; 6:19; Col. 1:26; 2:2; 2 Thess. 2:7; 1 Tim. 3:9; Rev. 17:5.

Acts 4:31 Updated American Standard Version (UASV)

³¹ And when they had prayed, the place in which they were gathered together was shaken, and they were all filled with the Holy Spirit and began to **speak the word of God with boldness.**

Just three days before Jesus was executed, Jesus told his disciples, "And this gospel of the kingdom will be proclaimed in all the inhabited earth⁵³ as a testimony to all the nations, and then the end will come." (Matt. 24:14) Jesus would speak on this again just before he ascended to heaven; Jesus said to his disciples, "Go therefore and make disciples of all the nations … teaching them to observe all that I commanded you …" (Matt 28:19-20) Of course, being curious, they were asking him, "Lord, is it at this time you are restoring the kingdom to Israel?" He said to them, "It is not

---

⁵² **Mystery; Secret:** (Gr. *mystērion*) A sacred divine mystery or secret doctrine that lies with God alone, which is withheld from both the angelic body and humans, until the time he determines that it is to be revealed, and to those to whom he chooses to make it known.– Mark 4:11; Rom. 11:25; 16:25; 1 Cor. 2:1; 4:1; 13:2; 14:2; 15:51; Eph. 1:9; 6:19; Col. 1:26; 2:2; 2 Thess. 2:7; 1 Tim. 3:9; Rev. 17:5.

⁵³ Or *in the whole world*

for you to know times or seasons that the Father has fixed by his own authority. But you will receive power when the Holy Spirit has come upon you, and you will be my witnesses in both Jerusalem and in all Judea and Samaria, and to the extremity of the earth."–Acts 1:6-8

It has been and will be mentioned several times in this publication; Christianity has lost its way in the great commission of proclaiming the good news of the kingdom, teaching biblical truths, and making disciples, even in the face of centuries of intensified missionary work this is true. It is the mission of Christian Publishing House and this author that the first-century lifesaving work of evangelism is restored, so that, all Christians may play a role in making disciples. Therefore, it is tools like this publication and others by this author and other authors, which will enable any willing Christian to share biblical truths effectively within their family, their community, their workplace or their school, to make disciples. Within this chapter, we will cover how the Holy Spirit can enable us to be bold when we are sharing biblical truths with others.[54]

The Need to Be Bold

One can only imagine the joy of making a disciple for Christ, who, in turn, goes out to make disciples himself. Congregation Evangelists, be it male or female should be very involved in evangelizing their communities and helping the church members play their role at the basic levels of evangelism. There is nothing to say that one church could not have many within, who have the calling of an evangelist, which would and should be cultivated. However, like in the first-century, we in the twenty-first-century have many challenges that get in our way. Generally speaking, few today are eager to hear from God's Word, mostly because the majority have preconceived ideas about it (just a man's book, full of errors and contradictions, and the like); many are of the same mindset as those who were living the days of Noah. "For as in those days before the flood they were eating and drinking, marrying and giving in marriage, until the day that Noah entered the ark." (Matt. 24:38-39, NASB) Then, the apostle Peter warned,

2 Peter 3:3-4 Updated American Standard Version (UASV)

[3] Know this first of all, that in the last days ridiculers will come with their ridicule, following after their own desires, [4] and saying: "Where is this

---

[54] A recommend read EXPLAINING THE HOLY SPIRIT: Basic Bible Doctrines of the Christian Faith

http://www.christianpublishers.org/apps/webstore/products/show/6565103

promised coming[55] of his? For ever since the fathers fell asleep, all continues just as it was from the beginning of creation."

On these verses, David Walls writes, "**In the last days** refers to all the days between the first advent of the Messiah and the second advent. Characteristic of that time frame, however long it will be, is the fact that people will make fun of the doctrine of the Second Coming. **Scoffing** toward Christians is to express derision or scorn about a Christian or Christianity, the Bible, or God. It describes the characteristic attitude of the day toward the Second Coming. False teachers argued that the promise of the Second Coming had been delayed so long that we may safely conclude that it would never happen. As far as they could see, the world was going on just as it always had–people lived and died, but nothing really changed." (Walls and Anders 1996, p. 141) Today, we have false teachers on both sides of the second coming fence: (1) ones that scoff at the idea of Jesus' second coming and (2) those that act as though they are prophets of God, knowing the very day and hour.[56] However, we also have those that from liberal and moderate "Christianity" that ridicule, mock and oppose conservative Christianity. All of this, and we have not even gotten to those outside of Christianity, who also ridicule, mock and oppose the Almighty God and his Word, the Bible.

As true Christians, we may face ridicule, mocking and opposition from the governmental officials, the news and entertainment media, other religions, and the agnostics and atheists. However, even more, close to home, it may come from those that our children go to school with, their teachers or it may originate from those we work with, even from close family members. All of these people need to be evangelized to if we are to carry out the Great Commission of proclaiming and teaching God's Word, to make disciples for Christ. We need to evangelize those in false forms of "Christianity," the unbelievers and those in either of these categories, who are closer to us.

However, we face yet more challenges that are in our way. One such challenge is our human imperfection, i.e., our human weaknesses, such as shyness and fear of being ridiculed, mocked and opposed. Lastly, our greatest obstacle is our church leaders, who are failing to train us to be effective evangelizers in our communities. James, Jesus' half-brother, wrote, "One of you says to them [the poor], 'Go in peace, be warmed and filled," without giving them the things needed for the body, what good is that? So also faith by itself, if it does not have works, is dead." (Jam. 2:16-

---

[55] Or *presence* (Gr *parousia*), which denotes both an "arrival" and a consequent "presence with."

[56] A recommended read The SECOND COMING of CHRIST: Basic Bible Doctrines of the Christian Faith

http://www.christianpublishers.org/apps/webstore/products/show/5383701

17, ESV) This principle can be carried over to pastors, elders, priests, ministers, who say to their congregation, "**You** need to share the gospel in **your** community, so that **you** may help build up the church for Christ." All of this pointing the finger at them by using the second person pronoun, "**you**" repeatedly, and these leaders have not even given them the tools to be effective evangelists within their community. What good is that? Therefore, their supposed faith that the evangelism work will be done, but having no works of training such ones, means they have no genuine faith at all, it is dead. If we are to persist in sharing the Word of God, this will require that we have the tools to help us (i.e., this book and others like it), as well as boldness. In this chapter, we will focus on boldness.

Ephesians 6:19-20 Updated American Standard Version (UASV)

¹⁹ and for me, that a word may be given to me at the opening of my mouth **boldly**, to make known the mystery of the gospel, ²⁰ for which I am an ambassador in chains, that I may proclaim it **boldly**, as I ought to speak.

The Greek word, *parresia*, "boldness" in verse 19 has the sense of in boldness "in an evident or publicly known manner–'publicly, in an evident manner, well known.'"[57] The Greek word, *parresiazomai*, "boldly" in verse 19, is a "(derivative of *parresia* 'boldness,' 25.158) to speak openly about something and with complete confidence—'to speak boldly, to speak openly.'"[58] However, this boldness, confidence, courage, fearlessness does not give us a license to be blunt or rude to the ones we speak to, even if their demeanor is such. The apostle said to the Christians in Rome, "Never pay back evil for evil to anyone." (Rom. 12:17; See Col. 4:6, NASB) He went on to say, "If possible, so far as it depends on you, be at peace with all men." (Rom. 12:18, NASB) When we go about our evangelism work, sharing God's Word with others, we need to be bold in this hostile world, but it needs to be balanced with tact as well because our objective is not to offend the one we to whom we are witnessing.

To be sure, this sort of boldness calls for personal qualities that involve much effort that needs to be developed over time. We do not just wake up one morning and decide that we are going to be bold from here forward. In addition, we do not just read a couple of Bible verses about being bold, and then, we are all of a sudden able to be bold in our witnessing to others. "But after we [Paul and his companions] had already suffered and been mistreated in Philippi, as you know, **we had the boldness in our God** to speak to you the gospel of God amid much conflict." (1 Thess. 2:2) We today can acquire a similar boldness if we are hesitant, shy or nervous at the idea of speaking to others about the Word of God.

---

[57] Johannes P. Louw and Eugene Albert Nida, *Greek-English Lexicon of the New Testament: Based on Semantic Domains* (New York: United Bible Societies, 1996), 337.
[58] IBID., 398.

Paul and his traveling companions had boldness, which you can note he said in the above, "we had the boldness in our God." In other words, God removed Paul's fears and gave him boldness. The rulers, elders, and scribes gathered in Jerusalem and commanded Peter and John to no longer witness about Jesus. These Jewish religious leaders had the power of life and death over them. Of course, they could only take their life, not their opportunity at eternal life. However, Peter and John answered them, "Whether it is right in the sight of God to listen to you rather than to God, you must judge, for we cannot but speak of what we have seen and heard." God was well aware of these threats, but he granted his servants to speak his word "*with all boldness.*" Ac 4:5, 19-20, 29, ESV) The Father had provided them with Holy Spirit. What about us; Should we expect that the Holy Spirit under this direct and supernatural control will guide, lead, and direct us in the same bold way.

What Was the Reason for the Direct and Supernatural Work of the Holy Spirit in the First Century?

A significant change was in the offing. The Jews had followed the lead of their religious leaders in the last act of rebellion, resulting in their rejection as his people. The Mosaic Law was being replaced with the law of Christ. This does not mean that no Jew could be received into the newly founded Christian congregation. To the contrary, the next three and half years would be only the Jewish people, which would make up this new way to God. As was the case with Moses, there was to be a sign, miraculous events, which included the speaking in tongues, this as evidence to those, whose heart was receptive to the truth that the Son of God had come, had given his life for them, and ascended back to heaven. Exodus 19:16-19

However, there was much labor to be done. Beginning in 36 C.E., with the conversion of Cornelius, an uncircumcised Gentile, the gospel got underway in its spread to non-Jewish people of every nation. (Acts, chap. 10) In truth, so swiftly did it spread that by about 60 C.E., the apostle Paul could say that the gospel had been "proclaimed in all creation that is under heaven." (Col. 1:23) Consequently, by the time of the last apostle's death (John c. 100 C.E.), Jesus' faithful followers had made disciples all the way through the Roman Empire—in Asia, Europe, and Africa! By 125 C.E., there were over one million Christians.

If we objectively look at the history of first-century Christianity, the three and a half year ministry of Jesus, founding the Christian congregation, the apostles spreading the good news throughout the whole of the Roman Empire, and the Holy Spirit miraculously guiding, leading and showing the apostles the "things to come," reminding them of all that Jesus had said. The apostles and a select few of others, like Paul, Barnabas, Silas, Apollos, Timothy, Titus, Philip, were under direct and supernatural control as they established Christianity in the first century. While there may have been a few individuals, attempting to cause division in the first century, by 100 C.E. there was but one Christianity, the one Jesus founded, and the apostle grew. The twenty-seven books of the New Testament were to be added to the Old Testament by 200 C.E. The particular work of the Holy Spirit that Jesus spoke of had run its course by the death of the apostle John in 100 C.E., as he was the last apostle. After John, no man has been miraculously guided or directed, in the same manner, and way, because that same specific work of the Holy Spirit was no longer needed. The work of the Holy Spirit from the second century forward has been within the inspired, inerrant Word of God. There was no need for the Holy Spirit to operate the same as in the first century because the work of setting up Christianity and completing the Word of God was completed. The work of the Holy Spirit now takes place through the Spirit-inspired Word of God.

What Were the Gifts of the Holy Spirit in the First-Century?

What miraculous, supernatural gifts were the apostles and a select few workers to receive, to establish first-century Christianity? They would receive a helper, comforter, an instructor, a guide, a supporter, i.e., the Holy Spirit. What did Jesus say about the Holy Spirit, being specifically applied to the apostles and a select few other fellow workers, to accomplish their work of establishing Christianity and completing the Bible? He had much to say on this, as we will discover from the texts below. Italics and underlines are mine.

John 14:15-17 Updated American Standard Version (UASV)

15 "If you love me, you will keep my commandments. 16 And I will ask the Father, and he will give you another Helper, that he may be with you forever; 17 the Spirit of truth, *whom the world cannot receive*, because it does not see him or know him, but you know him because *he dwells with you* and *will be in you*.

John 14:26 Updated American Standard Version (UASV)

26 But the Helper, the Holy Spirit, whom the Father will send in my name, *that one will teach you all things* and *bring to your remembrance all that I have said to you.*

John 15:26 Updated American Standard Version (UASV)

26 "But when the Helper comes, whom I will send to you from the Father, the Spirit of truth, who proceeds from the Father, *that one will bear witness about me.*

This took place with the apostles starting at Pentecost 33 C.E., as well as other Christians throughout the first-century.

John 16:5-8 Updated American Standard Version (UASV)

⁵ But now I am going to him who sent me, and none of you asks me, 'Where are you going?' ⁶ But because I have said these things to you, sorrow has filled your heart. ⁷ Nevertheless, I tell you the truth: it is to your advantage that I go away; for if I do not go away, the Helper will not come to you; but if I go, I will send him to you. ⁸ And when that one arrives, *he will convict the world concerning sin* and *righteousness* and *judgment*;

John 16:12-15 Updated American Standard Version (UASV)

¹² "I still have many things to say to you, but you cannot bear them now. ¹³ But when that one, the Spirit of truth, comes, *he will guide you into all the truth*; for he will not speak from himself, but whatever he hears, he will speak; and *he will declare to you the things that are to come.* ¹⁴ That one will glorify me, for *he will take what is mine and declare it to you.* ¹⁵ All the things that the Father has are mine; therefore I said that he takes what is mine and will declare it to you.

In the above texts, we have some things that the Holy Spirit was to do for the apostles and a select few other fellow workers. While the apostle was not ignorant or illiterate as some commentators suppose, they did not possess training in the Rabbinic study of Scripture, such as the apostle Paul had under Gamaliel. Luke tells us of an account of Peter and John before the Jewish religious leaders, where he writes,

Acts 4:13 Updated American Standard Version (UASV)

¹³ Now when they saw the boldness of Peter and John, and perceived that they were uneducated and untrained men, **they were astonished**, and they recognized that they had been with Jesus.

All of a sudden, Peter and John, literate fishermen were keeping pace with the Jewish religious leaders, who had training in the Rabbinic study of Scripture. This is the Holy Spirit teaching them, guiding them, instructing them, bringing back to their remembrance all that Jesus had said. Therefore, the apostles and a select few fellow workers needed the Holy Spirit if they were to establish Christianity on the grand scale that it was by the end of the first century and complete the New Testament. There was no way that the apostles alone could have educated themselves to the level of Paul, in such a short period, it was the Holy Spirit, who taught and instructed them miraculously. The Holy Spirit guided them as well. One way was in their writings, as no New Testament author contradicted another; they were all one because there was really one author, God. This is actually true of all forty plus authors of the entire Bible. From the second century forward, this has never repeated. In fact, today we have 41,000 different denominations, all teaching different things on the same doctrines.

Convicting the World Concerning Sin

Nisan 14, 33 C.E., the night of the Passover feast with Jesus, he told the apostles, "When he [the Holy Spirit] comes, he will convict the world concerning sin and righteousness and judgment." (John 16:8, ESV) How did the Holy Spirit do this on Pentecost? The first stage was to baptize the apostle in Holy Spirit, which means that they would have been miraculously endowed with guidance, instruction, teachings, and a remembrance of what Jesus had said. Again, looking at Jesus' words just before his ascension, he said, "for John baptized with water, but you will be baptized with the Holy Spirit not many days from now." (Acts 1:5, ESV) The second stage was the work that these ones would carry out in the first century, namely, putting the world on notice (convicting them concerning their sin and righteousness), which was very similar to what the Mosaic Law had done with the Israelites. Remember the words of the apostle Paul,

Romans 5:20-21 Updated American Standard Version (UASV)

[20] The [Mosaic] Law came in so that the transgression would increase; but where sin increased, grace abounded all the more, [21] so that, as sin reigned in death, even so grace would reign through righteousness to eternal life through Jesus Christ our Lord.

How did the Mosaic Law make sin "increase"? From Adam's rebellion to the Mosaic Law, man was well aware of right and wrong because even in imperfection he had a sense of right and wrong. God had given Adam and Eve a conscience, an internal mechanism, to evidence the difference between right and wrong. In their perfection, they were able to sin still because even if a perfect person entertains bad thoughts, it will lead to sin and death. (Jam 1:14-15) Nevertheless, humankind in imperfection has a measure of that conscience that was given to Adam and Eve, meaning they have always had a sense of good and bad. However, the Mosaic Law laid our more explicitly what sin was and the different aspects of it. The Pentateuch itself contained 613 laws. It was a theocratic government, covering religious obligations, duties of the priesthood, a judicial system, covering business, marriage, family, sexual relations, morality, military, dietary restrictions, sanitary laws and much more. Therefore, the Mosaic Law caused sin to increase. On this Paul wrote,

Romans 7:7-8 Updated American Standard Version (UASV)

[7] What shall we say then? Is the Law sin? May it never be! On the contrary, I would not have come to know sin except through the Law; for I would not have known about coveting if the Law had not said, "You shall not covet." [8] But sin, taking opportunity through the commandment, produced in me coveting of every kind; for apart from the Law sin is dead.

Like the apostle Paul, neither Jewish persons nor us today would know the full range of sin without the Mosaic Law. Paul gave us the example of coveting. The law exposed the coveting spirit that Paul would never have truly recognized in its fullest sense. This is how Paul could say, "apart from the Law sin *is* dead," specifically, it would not be as recognizable, as exposed, as highlighted. The Law made people more aware of the extent of their sinful nature. We should offer a word of caution, though, the Mosaic Law did not move them toward sin or make sin more appealing, but rather it exposed sin for what it was. Sin is missing the mark of perfection. Sin is being out of harmony with the Creator, his personality, standards, and ways, which he inculcated in his creation. The Law made it possible to convict more people concerning sin. Now, the apostles, baptized in Holy Spirit were going to take this a step further with the law of Christ. Again, Jesus said to his apostles, "When he [the Holy Spirit] comes, he will convict the world [by way of the apostle workers] concerning sin and righteousness and judgment." (John 16:8, ESV)

What do we mean by 'convicting the world concerning sin'? This is not a reference to sin in general, as though, the Holy Spirit would personally come upon a person who just watched a movie they should not have, or they just told a lie, or they committed any sin. When we feel this inner guilt, a groaning of our inner person, because we know we have just done wrong, this is not the Holy Spirit convicting us of that sin. It is the Holy Spirit working through the Word of God, which convicts us of sin. Sin will cause us to feel guilt, anxiety, insecurity, shame. We get a clearer understanding of this when we consider Paul's words that "the work of the law is written on their hearts, while their conscience also bears witness, and their conflicting thoughts accuse or even excuse them." (Rom 2:15, ESV) In other words, when we fall short of God's standards as they are laid out in Scripture or our God-given conscience, we will feel an internal groaning within us, which is our conscience convicting us of wrongdoing.

We are born with the weaker version of the conscience that God had given Adam and Eve. It will prevent most humans from committing the obvious right and wrongs, even if they never read the Word of God their entire life. However, considering that almost all of the teachers and professors in the United States and Especially Europe and Canada are of a liberal progressive mindset, which is contrary to God's standards, the conscience is greatly weakened by Satan's world. If our conscience is ignored, it will become calloused and unfeeling, no longer warning us of our wrongdoing because it is no longer wrongdoing in our heart and mind. On the other hand, if Scripture trains our conscience, it will not allow us to commit the wrongdoing in the first place. Returning to the being made bold by the Holy Spirit, we too can receive the Spirit in our evangelism work, but not in the same way and the same sense as the apostles and their fellow workers.

The Work of the Holy Spirit in the First Century

There was a different level of relationship between first-century Christianity and Christianity over the next 2,000 years. It must be remembered that Christ needed (1) **to train** those that would, (2) **establish Christianity**, and (3) **grow Christianity** to the point that it was **extensive and united**. This was needed to withstand the apostasy and false teachers that were to come over the next 2,000 years, who would split Christianity into so many factions, finding the truth and the way of the first century today is nigh impossible. All that Jesus and his apostles were to accomplish took place in a mere one hundred years while also publishing the twenty-seven books of the New Testament that later Christians would bring together as one book. There was a definite need for the Holy Spirit in first century Christianity. Let us look at the gifts of prophecy and speaking in tongues.

As for Tongues, They Will Cease

1 Corinthians 13:8-10 Updated American Standard Version (UASV)

8 Love never fails. But if there are gifts of prophecy, they will be done away with; if there are tongues,[59] they will cease; if there is knowledge, it will be done away with. 9 For we have partial knowledge and we prophesy partially, 10 but when what is complete comes, what is partial will be done away.

Some may argue that the evidence does not give one any idea of when the gift of tongues was to end. However, they would be mistaken in this case. There are three lines of evidence that present the fact that the gift of tongues would die out shortly after the death of the last apostle, which was the apostle John, who died about 98-100 C.E. **First**, the gift of tongues was always passed on to the person, only by an apostle: either by laying his hands on this one, or at least being present. (Acts 2:4, 14, 17; 10:44-46; 19:6; see also Acts 8:14-18.) **Second**, 1 Corinthians 13:8 informed the Corinthian reader specifically that this gift would "cease." In short, the Greek word for cease [*pausontai*], means to 'peter out,' or 'to die out,' not to be brought to a halt. We will deal with *pausontai* more extensively in a moment. **Third**, both one and two are exactly what happened when we look at the history of this gift of tongues. M'Clintock and Strong's *Cyclopaedia* (Vol. VI, p. 320) says that it is "an uncontested statement that

---

59 Namely, miraculous speaking in other languages.

during the first hundred years after the death of the apostles we hear little or nothing of the working of miracles by the early Christians." Therefore, following their passing off the scene and after those who in that way had obtained the gift of tongues breathed their last breath; the gift of tongues should have died out with these ones. (Elwell, 2001, 1207-8) This analysis concurs with the intention of those gifts as acknowledged at Hebrews 2:2-4. In other words, The gifts of the Spirit in the first century, which includes speaking in tongues, was evidence that God had abandoned the 1,600 years of the nation of Israel being the way to God to the Christian congregation.

Daniel B. Wallace in his *Greek Grammar Beyond the Basics* helps us to better comprehend how we are to understand *pausontai* of 1 Corinthians 13:8:

> If the voice of the verb here is significant, then Paul is saying either that tongues will cut themselves off (direct middle) or, more likely, cease of their own accord, i.e., 'die out' without an intervening agent (indirect middle). It may be significant with reference to prophecy and knowledge, Paul used a different verb ([*katargeo*]) and out it in the passive voice. In vv 9-10, the argument continues: 'for we *know* in part and we *prophecy* in part; but when the perfect comes, the partial shall be done away with [*katargethesontai*].' Here again, Paul uses the same passive verb he had used with prophecy and knowledge and he speaks of the verbal counterpart to the nominal 'prophecy' and 'knowledge.' Yet he does not speak about *tongues* being done away 'when the perfect comes.' The implication *may* be that tongues were to have 'died out' on their own *before* the perfect comes. (Wallace 1996, 422)

These abilities were only established by the presence or laying on of hands by the apostles. This coincides with 1 Corinthians 13:8 and the history of these phenomena. Our Greek word for "cease" means that the gift of tongues was to 'die out' over time as the last of those who had received this gift passed off the scene of this earth. This is established by the historical fact that the second century saw just that being evidenced. Today, the Christian is moved by Spirit to speak with his heart and mind, defending and establishing the gospel, and destroying false doctrines, snatching some back from the fire. It is these things, which will give credence to the words of the modern-day Christian congregation: "God is really among you."–1 Corinthians 14:24-25.

The special, supernatural gifts, such as speaking in tongues gave impetus to the evangelism work that needed to be done in the first century, into many different lands throughout the Roman Empire. (Matt 28:19-20; Ac 1:8; 2:1-11) In the first century, the ones who spoke in tongues did so in languages that others could understand. (Ac 2:4, 8) If we look at those who claim to do so today, it is some ecstatic explosion of incomprehensible sounds, which only draws attention to them.

1 Corinthians 12:7-11 Updated American Standard Version (UASV)

7 But the manifestation of the Spirit is given to each one for a beneficial purpose. 8 For to one is given speech of wisdom through the Spirit, to another speech of knowledge according to the same Spirit, 9 to another faith by the same Spirit, to another gifts of healing by that one Spirit, 10 to yet another operations of miraculous powers, to another prophesying, to another the distinguishing of spirits, to another different tongues, and to another interpretation of tongues. 11 But all these operations are performed by the very same Spirit, distributing to each one respectively just as it wills.

What we see here mentioned by Paul, apparently does not take place today in any Christian congregation. He is indicating various direct and supernatural manifestations of the Spirit, which was a direct gift from the Holy Spirit. There was a reason for these miraculous gifts, which Paul mentions in his letter to the Ephesians,

Ephesians 4:11-13 Updated American Standard Version (UASV)

11 And he gave some as apostles, and some as prophets, and some as evangelists, and some as shepherds and teachers, 12 for the equipping of the holy ones or the work of ministry, to the building up of the body of Christ; 13 until we all attain to the unity of the faith, and of the knowledge of the Son of God, to a mature man, to the measure of the stature which belongs to the fullness of Christ.

If we look at the above mention history of the Christian congregation of the first century and what was accomplished, it perfectly fits Paul's reasons here. The reason for the direct gifts of the Holy Spirit was (1) **to train** those that would, (2) **establish Christianity**, and (3) **grow Christianity** to the point that it was **extensive** and **united**. This gift of the Spirit accompanied the baptism of the Spirit on the day of Pentecost. As has been mentioned, the 120 disciples in that upper room, grew to become a united, one denomination of Christianity, which numbered over one million all throughout the Roman Empire, after a mere century. Therefore, when Peter promised the gift of the Holy Spirit on the day of Pentecost, it **was not** to be universally given across the whole of Christianity until the return of Jesus Christ, applying to all who obeyed the Word of God. Rather, it was limited to those of the first century. Even so, it was the apostles and a select few fellow workers, who manifested the Holy Spirit in a supernatural way, by being miraculously taught, instructed, guided, and bringing to their remembrance exactly what Jesus taught for three and a half years, and what Jesus meant by the words that he used. Yes, there were a number, in the first century, who were used as apostles [those caring for many congregations], and some as prophets [those proclaiming God's Word], and some as evangelists [a proclaimer of the gospel or good news],[60] and some as shepherds [elders or overseers in the congregation] and teachers [those who teach within the congregation].

Philip the Evangelist

Philip preached the Word of God to the Samaritans in the city of Samaria after the great persecution arose following the death of Stephen.

Acts 8:12-17 Updated American Standard Version (UASV)

12 But when they believed Philip as he preached good news about the kingdom of God and the name of Jesus Christ, they were baptized, both men and women. 13 Simon himself also believed, and after being baptized, he continued with Philip; and he was amazed at seeing the signs and great powerful works taking place.

14 Now when the apostles in Jerusalem heard that Samaria had received the word of God, they sent them Peter and John, 15 who came down and prayed for them that they might receive the Holy Spirit. 16 for he had not yet fallen on any of them, but they had only been baptized in the name of the Lord Jesus. 17 Then they laid their hands on them, and they received the Holy Spirit.

What do we notice here? We have Philip, a very important and prominent evangelist, who took the good news to Samaria. He preached and baptized the Samaritans. Philip was endowed with Holy Spirit with six other men, who were selected for a particular service. "These [seven men] set before the apostles, and they prayed and **laid their hands on them.**" (Ac 6:6) We see that Philip was able to perform signs and great miracles. If the gift of the Holy Spirit was to be for all who accepted Jesus and was baptized, why did the Samaritans not receive the Spirit? Philip was not an apostle, meaning he could not confer the gift of the Spirit by laying hands on them, even though he had had hands laid on him, and he could perform signs and great miracles. Therefore, Peter and John were dispatched to Samaria, to lay hands on the Samaritans, so that "they might receive the Holy Spirit." It should be noted that the gifts of the Holy Spirit

---

[60] Basic Evangelism is planting seeds of truth and watering any seeds that have been planted. [In the basic sense of this word (*euaggelistes*), this would involve all Christians.] In some cases, it may be that one Christian planted the seeds, which were initially rejected, so he was left in a good way because the planter did not try to force the truth down his throat. However, sometime later he faces something in life that moves him to reconsider those seeds, and some other Christian waters what had already been planted. This evangelism can be carried out in all of the methods that are available: informal, house-to-house, street, and the like. What amount of time is invested in the evangelism work is up to each Christian to decide for themselves.

were **always** conveyed to others by the apostles of Jesus Christ (1) laying on of hands (2) or in their presence.

The Holy Spirit Falls on the Gentile

Cornelius was a Gentile an army officer (centurion, KJV), who commanded 100 soldiers. He was "a devout man" who "feared God with all his household, gave alms generously to the people, and prayed continually to God," "an upright and God-fearing man, who is well spoken of by the whole Jewish nation." About the ninth hour of the day, he saw clearly in a vision an angel of God come in and say to him, "Cornelius." And he stared at him in terror and said, "What is it, Lord?" And he said to him, "Your prayers and your alms have ascended as a memorial before God." The angel also told Cornelius, "send men to Joppa and bring one Simon who is called Peter." (Acts 10:1-22) Again, the gifts of the Holy Spirit were always conveyed to others by the apostles of Jesus Christ (1) laying on of hands (2) or in their presence.

Acts 10:44-48 Updated American Standard Version (UASV)

44 While Peter was still speaking these words, the Holy Spirit fell upon all who heard the word. 45 All the circumcised believers[61] who came with Peter were amazed, because the gift of the Holy Spirit had been poured out on the Gentiles also. 46 For they were hearing them speaking with tongues and magnifying God. Then Peter answered, 47 "Can anyone withhold water for baptizing these people, who have received the Holy Spirit just as we have?" 48 And he commanded them to be baptized in the name of Jesus Christ. Then they asked him to remain for some days.

Disciples at Ephesus

In Acts chapter 19, we find Paul meeting up with certain disciples that had been baptized by the John the Baptist. Paul explained that John was not aware of the full Gospel before his death. Below you will notice that these disciples of John had not even heard of the Holy Spirit, even though John pointed his disciples toward Jesus. Yet again, the gifts of the Holy Spirit were always conveyed to others by the apostles of Jesus Christ (1) laying on of hands (2) or in their presence.

Acts 19:1-7 English Standard Version (ESV)

1 And it happened that while Apollos was at Corinth, Paul passed through the inland country and came to Ephesus. There he found some disciples. 2 And he said to them, "Did you receive the Holy Spirit when you believed?" And they said, "No, we have not even heard that there is a Holy Spirit." 3 And he said, "Into what then were you baptized?" They said, "Into John's baptism." 4 And Paul said, "John baptized with the baptism of repentance, telling the people to believe in the one who was to

---

61 I.e., faithful ones

come after him, that is, Jesus." [5] On hearing this, they were baptized in the name of the Lord Jesus. [6] And when Paul had laid his hands on them, the Holy Spirit came on them, and they began speaking in tongues and prophesying. [7] There were about twelve men in all.

Young Timothy

Here is yet another experience where someone has received the Holy Spirit by an apostle laying hands on him or her. Once more, the gifts of the Holy Spirit were always conveyed to others by the apostles of Jesus Christ (1) laying on of hands (2) or in their presence.

2 Timothy 1:4-7 Updated American Standard Version (UASV)

[4] longing to see you, even as I recall your tears, so that I may be filled with joy; [5] having been reminded of[62] your unhypocritical faith, which first dwelt in your grandmother Lois and your mother Eunice, and I am sure that it is in you as well. [6] For this reason I remind you to kindle afresh the gift of God which is in you through the laying on of my hands. [7] For God did not give us a spirit of cowardice, but one of power and of love and of soundness of mind.[63]

Christians In Rome

That the gifts of the Holy Spirit were always conveyed to others by the apostles of Jesus Christ (1) laying on of hands (2) or in their presence was clear. Listen to the praise of Paul to these ones in Rome. He writes, "To all those in Rome who are loved by God and called to be holy ones: 'Grace to you and peace from God our Father and the Lord Jesus Christ. First, I thank my God through Jesus Christ for all of you, because your faith is proclaimed in all the world. For God is my witness, whom I serve with my spirit in the gospel of his Son, that without ceasing I mention you always in my prayers, asking that somehow by God's will I may now, at last, succeed in coming to you.'" Paul goes on to tell these Christians.

Romans 1:11 Updated American Standard Version (UASV)

[11] For I long to see you so that I may impart some spiritual gift to you, that you may be established;

Notice that Paul could encourage and counsel them from a distance in the longest letter he had penned. However, it was necessary that he be present to convey gifts of the Spirit by his presence or the laying on of hands.

---

[62] Lit *receiving a remembrance of*

[63] **Sound in Mind:** (Gr. *sophroneo*) This means to be of sound mind or in one's right mind, i.e., to have understanding about practical matters and thus be able to act sensibly, 'to have sound judgment, to be sensible, to use good sense, sound judgment.'–Acts 26:25; Romans 12:3; 2 Timothy 1:7; Titus 2:6; 1 Peter 4:7

What have we learned thus far? First, the gift of the Spirit was a miraculous, supernatural gift for helping the first-century believers to be bold, to perform signs and miracles, to speak in foreign languages, to be Jesus' "witnesses in Jerusalem and in all Judea and Samaria, and to the end of the earth." (Ac 1:8) We also notice that the gifts of the Holy Spirit were **always** conveyed to others by the apostles of Jesus Christ (1) laying on of hands (2) or in their presence. Moreover, once the last apostle died, John, in 100 C.E., there was no longer one available to convey the gifts of the Spirit.

Therefore, the Greek word at 1 Corinthians 13:8 for "cease" [pausontai], became a reality in that the gifts that had been given 'petered out,' or 'died out,' namely, they were not brought to a halt, as some were, like prophecy. In other words, they died out as the last ones who were given them died at the beginning of the second century. Second, we can see from the letters of the New Testament authors that in the first century, many of the congregations were filled with members that had the supernatural power of the Spirit. Moreover, when we interpret those letters, this must be a part of the historical setting. Below are a few examples of these letters,

Romans 8:9, 23 Updated American Standard Version (UASV)

⁹ However, you are not in the flesh but in the Spirit, if indeed **the Spirit of God dwells in you.** But if anyone does not have the Spirit of Christ, he does not belong to him. ²³ And not only this, but also we ourselves, having the **first fruits of the Spirit,** even we ourselves groan within ourselves, waiting eagerly for our adoption as sons, the redemption of our body.

Romans 15:30 Updated American Standard Version (UASV)

³⁰ Now I urge you, brothers, through our Lord Jesus Christ and through **the love of the Spirit,** that you exert yourselves with me in prayers to God for me,

2 Corinthians 5:5 Updated American Standard Version (UASV)

⁵ Now the one who prepared us for this very thing is God, who gave us **the Spirit as a down payment** of what is to come.

Ephesians 1:13-14 Updated American Standard Version (UASV)

¹³ In whom also, you having heard the word of truth, the gospel of your salvation, in whom also having trusted, were **sealed with the Holy Spirit** of promise, ¹⁴ who is a down payment of our inheritance for the redemption of the possession, to the praise of his glory.

Ephesians 2:18 Updated American Standard Version (UASV)

¹⁸ for through him we both have our **access in one Spirit** to the Father.

Ephesians 5:18 Updated American Standard Version (UASV)

[18] And do not get drunk with wine, for that is[64] dissipation,[65] but be **filled with the Spirit,**

1 Thessalonians 4:8 Updated American Standard Version (UASV)

[8] Therefore the one who rejects this is not rejecting man, but God, who also **gives his Holy Spirit to you.**

Titus 3:5 Updated American Standard Version (UASV)

[5] he saved us, not by deeds of righteousness that we have done, but because of his mercy, through the **washing** of **regeneration** and **renewal by the Holy Spirit,**

Hebrews 2:4 Updated American Standard Version (UASV)

[4] God also testifying with them, both by **signs** and **wonders** and by various **miracles** and by **gifts of the Holy Spirit** <u>according to His own will.</u>

James 4:5 Updated American Standard Version (UASV)

[5] Or do you think that the Scripture speaks to no purpose, "The **spirit that dwells in us** strongly desires to envy"?

1 John 2:20, 27 Updated American Standard Version (UASV)

[20] But you have been **anointed by the Holy One,** and you all have knowledge. [27] As for you, the **anointing which you received from him remains in you,** and you have no need for anyone to teach you; but as his anointing teaches you about all things, and is true and is not a lie, and just as it has taught you, you remain in him.

1 John 4:13 Updated American Standard Version (UASV)

[13] By this we know that we are remaining in him and he in us, because he has given **his Spirit to us.**

The Holy Spirit and Today's Christians

Can The Holy Spirit do the same for us? No, the Holy Spirit cannot, at least not in the same way and the same sense. How, then, can we receive the Holy Spirit, to be instructed, guide, taught, reminded and to be directed in our witnessing to others in our evangelism work? As an aside, the answer will apply to every other facet of our Christian life as well, we just happen to be focusing on the evangelism aspect. Let us look at the thought of the

---

[64] Lit *in which is*

[65] behavior which shows lack of concern or thought for the consequences of an action—'senseless deeds, reckless deeds, recklessness.'—GELNTBSD

Holy Spirit instructing and teaching Christians. Today we have over 41,000 different denominations, all teaching different doctrinal positions on the same subject matter. If we choose just one denomination, we find that each of the tens of thousands of pastors in the churches does not have to teach the same thing about the same doctrine. Then, let us take and one church within that denominations, and we will find that the church members do not all believe the same thing as their pastor.

Thus, we have all sorts of men teaching different views on every doctrine. Let us look at a few examples, so we can better understand. In dealing with the inspiration of God's Word, most church leaders teach The Infallibilist View, meaning that they believe the Bible is infallible only in matters of faith, but that it contains many mistakes, errors, and contradictions in matters when it touches on science, history, and geography. On the other hand, few conservative church leaders still teach The Inerrantist View, meaning that they believe the Bible is without error of any kind. On the doctrine of the atonement, some leaders have The Penal Substitution View, meaning that they believe that Christ died in our place. Others have the Christus Victor View, meaning that they believe Christ destroyed Satan and his works. While others have The Moral Government View, meaning that they believe Christ displayed God's wrath against sin. Concerning the doctrine of Sanctification, there are four main views. We have the Lutheran View, meaning sanctification as a declaration by God. We have the Calvinist view, meaning sanctification as holiness in Christ and personal conduct. Then, we have the Keswick View, meaning sanctification as resting-faith in the sufficiency of Christ. In addition, we have the Wesleyan, View, meaning entire sanctification as perfect love. Even these four beliefs on sanctification are not completely accepted because each church leader can tweak it to fit his understanding of things. These doctrines are just the beginning. We could cover The Providence Debate, i.e., the sovereignty of God. We could talk about different foreknowledge beliefs; the divine image differences the different salvation beliefs, the various beliefs about the human constitution, eternal security, the destiny of the evangelized, baptism, charismatic gifts, hellfire, and numerous others.

These differences in the Christian leader's beliefs are often contradictory. Are we to believe that the Holy Spirit one church leader to teach that sinners are destined to enteral torment in hellfire while other leaders teach eternal destruction for the sinners? Are we to believe that the Holy Spirit teaches different church leaders four different views on sanctification? The belief that the Holy Spirit is still carrying out the same work today as what the Father and the Son assigned in the first century, place the Holy Spirit in a very unenviable position, i.e., teaching different views on the same doctrine, some of which are even contradictory. Can we accept that the Holy Spirit teaches different views on all doctrinal positions, even being contradictory? Remember, it was the Holy Spirit, who taught and instructed the apostles miraculously. The Holy Spirit guided them as well. One way was in their writings, as no New Testament author contradicted another, they were all one because there was really one author, God. This is actually true of all forty plus authors of the entire Bible. Thus, we are to believe that the Holy Spirit moved over forty Bible authors miraculously, over a 1,600-year period, to pen sixty-six Bible books, in all of which there is not one contraction, error or mistake, but now the Holy Spirit is teaching different views and contradictory information? We would not say in the church of and leader, who taught contradictory information, so why would we accept that the Holy Spirit would do such a thing. Supposing that churches evangelized their own communities, which they do not, but let us suppose they did. How should an atheist feel if different churches came to his home to witness to him and they told him contradictory views about the same doctrine?

The problem is the belief that the Holy Spirit is carrying out the same work after that work was completed in the first century. Only the apostles and a select few fellow workers received the Holy Spirit in a direct and supernatural way, teaching them, guiding them, instructing them, bringing back to their remembrance all that Jesus had said. The apostle Paul told Timothy, "The things which you have heard from me in the presence of many witnesses, entrust these to faithful men who will be able to teach others also." (2 Tim. 2:2) We all know that Timothy traveled with Paul for 15 years, being taught by Paul (Paul already being extremely educated by Gamaliel), but more importantly, miraculously taught and instructed by the Holy Spirit. This clearly was not the case with Timothy (his being taught and instructed by the Holy Spirit in the same way and to the same extent), as Timothy was taught by Paul and his study of the Old Testament Scriptures. This text evidences that we are to be taught and instructed by Holy Spirit by way of our study the Holy, Spirit-inspired Scriptures.

If the Holy Spirit were miraculously teaching and instructing Christians today, as took place with the apostles and a select few fellow workers, there would be no need for any sort of Bible study tools, such as Bible dictionaries, encyclopedias, word study dictionaries, commentaries, and the like. Even so, while there are no direct Scriptures to evidence Timothy receiving Holy Spirit in the same way as Paul and the twelve apostles, we know that Holy Spirit led Paul to Timothy on his second missionary tour. We know that Paul saw something in Timothy that brought about a 15-year friendship and bond between the two like no other. Timothy became an extremely valuable co-worker of the apostle Paul, in a time, when the Holy Spirit was building the first-century Christian congregation. Therefore, we cannot discount the possibility that Timothy was guided by the Holy Spirit as Paul had been, maybe not to the same degree, and that he was not taught and instructed in the same way and sense but used more directly by the Holy Spirit than those after the first century, including us today. Let us get back to the apostles for a moment. Let us look at the apostles in the very beginning of Acts, as Jesus tells them,

Acts 1:8 Updated American Standard Version (UASV)

⁸ But you will receive power when **the Holy Spirit has come upon you;** and you will be my witnesses in both Jerusalem and in all Judea and Samaria, and to the extremity of the earth."

Earlier, Jesus had told them that he was going away and that he was sending them a helper, the Holy Spirit. Now, he specifically tells them, "You [namely, the apostles] will receive power when the Holy Spirit has come upon you, and you will be my witnesses in Jerusalem and in all Judea and Samaria, and to the end of the earth." Just after Jesus said these things, as they were watching, he ascended back to heaven to be with the Father. Some days later on Sivan 6, 33 C.E., they would receive the power of the Holy Spirit, where there was an outpouring of Holy Spirit. (Acts 2:1-17, 38) If they had already received the Holy Spirit, they would not have needed to call the brothers together to determine who was going to replace Judas as the twelfth apostle. Moreover, "they cast lots for them [Joseph called Barsabbas, who was also called Justus, and Matthias], and the lot fell on Matthias, and he was numbered with the eleven apostles."–Acts 1:15-26

Obtain Boldness

Jesus told his listeners,

Luke 11:13 Updated American Standard Version (UASV)

¹³ If you then, being evil, know how to give good gifts to your children, how much more will your heavenly Father give the Holy Spirit to those who ask Him?"

If we want to receive the Holy Spirit, we just go to the Father in prayer and ask him. If we want to be bolder in our sharing of the good news, we can pray to God for the Holy Spirit. However, we must not misunderstand the Scriptures, so as to expect the miraculous, supernatural gifts of the Holy Spirit in the same sense and the same way as the apostle, their fellow workers, and the Christians of the first century. If we want to become a better teacher in the Bible class at our churches, we will have to be a better Bible student, take in many Scriptures that deal with the principles of being a more effective teacher, put these into practice, and maybe pick up some good Christian books on being a better teacher. In this way, we would be working in harmony with our prayer, because the Word of God is Spirit inspired, and thus the more we delve into it and apply it in a correct and balanced manner; in essence, we are getting more Holy Spirit. If we want to teach the Bible to the Spanish-speaking people in our community, we may want to learn the Spanish language.

Some might believe that I am suggesting that the Holy Spirit is not active today. This is not the case. It is not the question of whether the Spirit is active, but how the Spirit is active. We can all agree that the Holy Spirit is pleading with the unsaved world, to help them find the path of salvation that leads to accepting Jesus Christ. This is not accomplished in some miraculous, supernatural way, but rather through our work as ambassadors for Christ. New Testament Bible scholar Richard L. Pratt Jr., made the following comment on 1 Corinthians 5:20a,

> Paul's role in the divine plan of reconciliation led him to a remarkable claim. He and his company were **Christ's ambassadors.** "Ambassadors" was a technical political term used in Paul's day that closely parallels our English word "ambassadors." An ambassador represented a nation or kingdom in communication with other nations. Paul had in mind his apostolic call to represent the kingdom of Christ to the nations of the earth. Ambassadors held positions of great honor in the ancient world because they represented the authority of the kings on whose behalf they spoke.
>
> This was also true for Paul as the ambassador of Christ. When he spoke the message of reconciliation, it was **as though God were making his appeal through** him. Rather than speaking directly to the nations of earth, God ordained that human spokespersons would speak for him. As an apostle, Paul had authority to lead and guide the church (2 Cor. 13:3, 10). Yet, this description applies to all who bear the gospel of Christ to others—even to those who do not bear apostolic authority (1 Pet. 4:11). Though we may not present the gospel as perfectly as Paul did, we do speak on God's behalf when we bring the message of grace to others. But Paul and his company were to be received as mouthpieces of God in the most authoritative sense. (Pratt Jr 2000, p. 359)

2 Corinthians 5:16-20 Updated American Standard Version (UASV)

[16] From now on, therefore, we regard no one according to the flesh. Even though we once regarded Christ according to the flesh, we regard him thus no longer. [17] Therefore if anyone is in Christ, he is a new creation; the old things have passed away; behold, new things have come. [18] And all

these things are from God, who has reconciled us to himself through Christ, and who has given us the ministry of reconciliation, [19] namely, that God was in Christ reconciling the world to himself, not counting their trespasses against them, and entrusting to us the message of reconciliation. [20] Therefore, we are ambassadors for Christ, as though God were making an appeal through us; we beg you on behalf of Christ, be reconciled to God.

As ambassadors for Christ, we are not seeking to offer superficial feel-good solutions to the problems of their imperfection, nor the wicked world in which we live. We are not telling them that, if they accept Christ, God will take care of their problems, and they will feel better about life. Sadly, many who first come to a Christian meeting are looking for just that; they want God to help them cope with the imperfection that surrounds their every waking moment. We certainly can counsel them biblically, which will enable them to improve their lot in life, will help them be stronger in dealing with this imperfection we all face, and, generally speaking, if they live a Christlike life, there will be fewer problems that a worldly life. However, our serving as ambassadors for Christ, this is not the goal of our service to the unbelieving world. We are offering them the same gospel that Paul did. In other words, the Father loved the world of humankind so much, he offered the only begotten Son, and the Father is willing to forgive any of their Adamic, inherited sin, by means of Christ Jesus. Paul wrote,

Romans 5:10-12, 8:32 Updated American Standard Version (UASV)

[10] For if while we were enemies we were **reconciled to God** through the death of his Son, much more, having been **reconciled**, we shall be saved by his life. [11] Not only that, but we are also exulting in God through our Lord Jesus Christ, through whom we have now received the **reconciliation.**

[12] Therefore, just as through one man sin entered into the world, and death through sin, and so death spread to all men, because all sinned,

[32] He who did not spare his own Son, but delivered him over for us all, how will he not also with him freely give us all things?

To reconcile means to "restore to friendship or harmony."[66] The Greek *katallasso* means, "'to reconcile.' It is related to the Greek word, *allasso,* which means, "to change, exchange" (6x in the NT: Acts 6:14; Rom 1:23; 1 Cor. 15:51–52; Gal 4:20; Heb. 1:12)."[67] In the New Testament, *katallasso* "is a theological term describing the removal of enmity between humans and God (Rom. 5:10 [2x], 2 Cor. 5:18, 19, 20); it

---

[66] Frederick C. Mish, "Preface," *Merriam-Webster's Collegiate Dictionary.* (Springfield, MA: Merriam-Webster, Inc., 2003).

[67] William D. Mounce, Mounce's Complete Expository Dictionary of Old & New Testament Words (Grand Rapids, MI: Zondervan, 2006), 565.

occurs only once in reference to human relationships (1 Cor. 7:11, husband/wife; it is significant that marriage is the relationship chosen for the use of this word). In biblical thought, God reconciles humans to himself through the death of his Son (Rom 5:10; 2 Cor. 5:18–20)."[68]

Reconciliation to God

The Greek word *katallage* in the New Testament is used "for our 'reconciliation' with God, which has taken place through Christ's blood (Rom. 5:11). It is, therefore, a work of God in that he is the one who removes the enmity between himself and humanity (2 Cor. 5:18–19). This divine act does require a response of faith from the human beings. This is why Paul admonishes his readers to 'be reconciled to God' (2 Cor. 5:20; see reconcile). The majority of Jews made reconciliation available to all people because of their rejection of Christ (Rom. 11:15). Now, this is not to say that non-Jews were never going to benefit from the ransom as that was already part of the will and purposes of God from Genesis 3:15 forward. Such removal of enmity between God and the human race should lead to missionary zeal–to our being Christ's ambassadors (2 Cor. 5:20)."[69]

The apostle Paul tells us why reconciliation to God is needed when he writes, "sin came into the world through one man, and death through sin, and so death spread to all men because all sinned." (Rom. 5:12, ESV) Since Adam and Eve rebelled and were expelled from the Garden of Eden, there has been this alienation between man and God, a separation, a lack of harmony with God's personality, standards, ways, and will. In fact, humanity has been in a state of hostility toward God. Paul wrote, "For the mind that is set on the flesh is hostile to God, for it does not submit to God's law; indeed, it cannot. Those who are in the flesh cannot please God." (Rom. 8:7-8, ESV) When Paul says, "those who are in the flesh cannot please God," he is not referring to literal human flesh, as this is the very condition in which he created humans. Paul's use of "flesh" here is a reference to our fallen condition as imperfect humans with inherited sinful tendencies.

If we are to be truly forgiven of our Adamic sin, namely, our inherited sin, and any sin we make commit while in human imperfection, we must repent and ask for forgiveness. Even, though, it is the Christian, who is repenting, turning to God, he must realize it is not his insight, his goodness but rather God who is drawing him. By the Word of God, the unbeliever will come to recognize that he needs to be forgiven, which can only come by and through Christ's atonement sacrifice. Christians, while they are still

---

[68] IBID., 566
[69] IBID., 566

in imperfection, suffering from human weaknesses, sin-laden flesh, they can still be declared righteous (namely, credited righteousness) because of the merits of the sacrifice of Jesus Christ being applied on their behalf. They then have a righteous, uncondemned standing before God. The Father has given Christians the most precious gift he could, his own begotten Son for his worshipers. God can declare righteous all who accept his Son, Jesus Christ. They will become new persons, who are at peace with God. (Eph. 4:22-24; Col. 3:9-10) How is it possible for persons such as Abel, Noah, Abraham, Moses, Joshua, David and others from pre-Christian times to be reconciled to God and declared righteous when they died before Jesus' ransom sacrifice? The apostle Paul writes, "By faith Abel offered to God a better sacrifice than Cain, through which he obtained the testimony that **he was righteous**, God testifying about his gifts." (Heb. 11:4-5, NASB) James writes, "The Scripture was fulfilled which says, 'And Abraham believed God, and it was **reckoned to him as righteousness**,' and he was called the friend of God.'" (Jam. 2:23, NASB) Even John the Baptist died before Jesus had offered himself as a ransom sacrifice. If God had already dealt with these ones and blessed, why would they need reconciliation by means of Jesus' sacrifice? Let us first take an excursion to look at how they were declared righteous.

EPHESIANS 6:20

By Edward D. Andrews

Ephesians 6:20 Updated American Standard Version (UASV)

20 for which I am an ambassador in chains;[70] that in it **I may speak boldly,** as I ought to speak.

Using God's Word with Persuasion

A confusion that arises over using the Bible effectively when witnessing to others is the belief that, it is simply boils down to knowing and quoting Scripture. What do we read of the way the apostle Paul went about witnessing to others? It says, "He entered the synagogue and for three months **spoke boldly, reasoning** and **persuading** them." (Ac 19:8-9) On another occasion, "when some became stubborn and continued in unbelief, speaking evil of the Way before the congregation, he withdrew from them and took the disciples with him, **reasoning** daily in the hall of Tyrannus." Persuasion is "attempting to win others over to one's own point of view. It can be either positive, as with preaching the gospel, or it can spring from a malign intent to seduce people from the truth." (Manser 2009) When one is persuaded, he is won over by the ability of the persuader's reasoning, arguments (reasons put forward in support), explaining of the Scriptures, i.e., he is so convinced that he gains confidence in God's Word. When Christians persuade a person to accept the Bible as the inspired, inerrant Word of God, we are winning him over, so that he will place his trust in the Bible. If we are to accomplish this in the skeptical, atheistic, agnostic, humanistic, liberal, progressive world that we live in, we must possess the skills to teach our listeners of the truthfulness of our reasons we put forward in support of the biblical worldview, or rather in opposition to the fleshly worldview of today's' hedonistic society.

We do not want to shy away from using God's Word; because that just demonstrates that, we have a lack of respect for it. The modern-day critic of the 20th and 21st centuries has taken over in the driving of the conversation, and it is he who decides what is evidence and what is not. The critic's conclusion is that Bible manuscripts that date back 2,300 years are not historical, archaeological evidence, but rather are biased material and if we cannot offer up secular evidence for what we say; well then, we have no evidence at all. The modern-day Bible scholar has chosen to play by the critic's rules of engagement, so they actually run around looking for

---

70 Lit *a chain*

ways to prove things with secular history alone. First, we do not cower before Satan and his people, leaving them to determine whether we can draw attention to God's Word. It is certainly beneficial and appropriate that our great apologetic arguers, like Norman L. Geisler, William Lane Craig, or Craig Evans defend the truth against the lies of the great minds of Satan's side. However, our primary commission is winning the hearts and minds of those receptive to the truth, not winning arguments against those who will never accept the truth, regardless of the evidence.[71]

Therefore, we need to be quite familiar with the Word of God and know what the authors meant by the words that they used. Whether we open our Bible to share a Scripture or reference it aloud, draw attention to the importance of what God's thinking is on the subject that we may be discussing. After a very brief introduction and our mission of sharing God's Word, we might open with an open-ended question. We might say, fifty percent of marriages in America fail, and then ask, "Why do you think that is?" [Allow for an answer] How do you think this principle from God's Word would help, Paul said, "Let no one seek his own good, but the good of his neighbor." (1 Cor. 10.24, ESV) If both mates were to seek the good of the other, how might we see that playing out, can you think of any examples? [Allow for an answer] If the person is receptive, offer a couple more Bible principles that deal with spouses that seem to be growing apart (Phil 1:10), mates that fail to fulfill their responsibilities (Rom 14:12), the husband that seems to not care where the family is heading (Pro. 14:1) habits that annoy one another (Col. 3:13), and so on.

We need to reason from the Scripture where we leave our listeners with no doubt whatsoever that what they are hearing is the truth. Therefore, we need to use genuine, warm, earnest, profound and honest entreaty, with sound logic. As Jesus and Paul, our objective is to reach the heart of those to whom we witness. This is realized in the words of wise King Solomon, "The purpose in a man's heart is like deep water, but a man of understanding will draw it out." (Pro. 20:5) Yes, we need to draw out what is in the heart of our listener, by using kind, loving and respectful questions that evidence we are personally interested in them. We must avoid being too direct and frank. In other words, we do not want to have a cutting edge to our questions, nor do we want to be too frank or straightforward and showing no delicacy or consideration when using questions. When we are making arguments to substantiate a point, make them clear and logical. We want to offer evidence that will satisfy the

---

[71] Keep in mind that when Geisler, Craig and Evans are debating to on stage against a atheist scientist or the like; they are talking past him, if he is unreceptive to any in the audience that may be receptive. It is evidence that we have answers in the conversation, whether they want to hear them or not, so that unbelievers can see that we do have reasonable, logical answers to the deep questions that plague humanity.

listener. Moreover, we want to share what the Bible author meant by the use of his words, not what we think he meant. Time is critical and should be used judiciously. Rather than rush through reading three or four verses that make our point, we should choose the clearest one, use it well by explaining, reasoning and illustrating. When we think of using corroborative evidence, again, we turn to Solomon, "From a wise mind comes wise speech; the words of the wise are persuasive." (Pro. 16:23, NLT) If there is a need for more research on our part, say so, by stating that we will look into this further and get back to them another time.

Carry on Using God's Word Skillfully

The world is ever changing toward being more wicked each and every day. In fact, Paul told Timothy, "Evil people and impostors will go on from bad to worse, deceiving and being deceived." (2 Tim. 3:13) Thus, 2,000 years later this is even truer. Therefore, it is highly significant that "we destroy arguments and every lofty opinion raised against the knowledge of God, and take every thought captive to obey Christ." We do this by using "the sword of the Spirit, which is the word of God."–(Eph. 6:17) As the author of Hebrews tells us, "For the word of God is living and active, sharper than any two-edged sword, piercing to the division of soul and of spirit, of joints and of marrow, and discerning the thoughts and intentions of the heart." (Heb. 4:12, ESV) Jesus words ring true, "For what will it profit a man if he gains the whole world and forfeits his soul? Or what will a man give in exchange for his soul?" – Matthew 16:26, NASB.

1 Peter 1:13-15 Updated American Standard Version (UASV)

[13] Therefore, gird the loins of your mind,[72] and being sober-minded,[73] set your hope fully on the grace that will be brought to you at the revelation of Jesus Christ. [14] As children of obedience,[74] do not be conformed according to the desires you formerly had in your ignorance, [15] but like the Holy One who called you, you also be holy in all your conduct; [16] because it is written, "You shall be holy, for I am holy."

Defending the Hope That Is In You

We must begin with the fact that we must know accurately what the Bible says on different Bible doctrines and be able to offer substantial reasons for the faith. As to the biblical truths, we do not want to remain a

---

[72] I.e., *prepare your minds for action (mental perception)*

[73] **Sober Minded:** (Gr. *nepho*) This denotes being sound in mind, to be in control of one's thought processes and thus not be in danger of irrational thinking, 'to be sober-minded, to be well composed in mind.'–1 Thessalonians 5:6, 8; 2 Timothy 4:5; 1 Peter 1:13; 4:7; 5:8

[74] I.e., *obedient children*

spiritual babe. "For everyone who partakes only of milk is not accustomed to the word of righteousness, for he is an infant. But solid food is for the mature, who because of practice have their senses trained to discern good and evil. Therefore, leaving the elementary teaching about the Christ, let us press on to maturity." (Hebrews 5:13-6:1) We can consider a Bible example of one, who lack a deeper knowledge, through no fault of his own, correcting it once it was brought to his attention, namely, Apollos. The account is below; notice how he can defend the faith much better after he received the way of God more accurately, he eagerly helps others discover this hope.

Acts 18:24-28 Updated American Standard Version (UASV)

²⁴ Now a certain Jew named Apollos, a native of Alexandria, an eloquent man, arrived in Ephesus; and he was well versed in the Scriptures. ²⁵ This man had been orally instructed in the way of the Lord; and being fervent in spirit, he was speaking and teaching accurately the things concerning Jesus, being acquainted only with the baptism of John; ²⁶ and this man began to speak out boldly in the synagogue. But when Priscilla and Aquila heard him, they took him aside and explained to him the way of God more accurately. ²⁷ And when he wanted to go across to Achaia, the brothers encouraged him and wrote to the disciples to welcome him; and when he had arrived, he greatly helped those who had believed through grace, ²⁸ for he powerfully refuted the Jews in public, demonstrating by the Scriptures that Jesus was the Christ.

Just as was true of Priscilla and Aquila, Christian evangelists should be able to share the faith accurately to unbelievers, to those who have started to doubt, and to those in Christian denominations that are not on the true path of salvation. If we are to accomplish these things, we must have an accurate, full, true knowledge of God's Word. Paul wrote to the brothers in Colossae, "For this reason also, since the day we heard of it, we have not ceased to pray for you and to ask that you may be filled with the accurate knowledge[75] of his will in all spiritual wisdom and understanding, so as to walk in a manner worthy of the Lord, fully pleasing to him bearing fruit in every good work and increasing in the accurate knowledge[76] of God." – Colossians 1:9-10

This sharing of the Gospel is not just some basic biblical truth of Jesus's life and ministry, death, resurrection, and ascension. Moreover, this is not

---

[75] *Epignosis* is a strengthened or intensified form of *gnosis* (*epi,* meaning "additional"), meaning, "true," "real," "full," "complete" or "accurate," depending upon the context. Paul and Peter alone use *epignosis.*

[76] *Epignosis* is a strengthened or intensified form of *gnosis* (*epi,* meaning "additional"), meaning, "true," "real," "full," "complete" or "accurate," depending upon the context. Paul and Peter alone use *epignosis.*

just being able to string many good sounding words together, but rather words that will lead others to the same hope that we hold so dearly. The principle behind Paul's words to the Corinthians makes this point nicely. He wrote, "I would rather speak five words with my mind in order to instruct others, than ten thousand words in a tongue." – 1 Corinthians 14:19

Yes, Christians looking to share biblical truths with others should seek to do so with words of understanding. They should possess an accurate, full and true knowledge about the Father, the Son, The Holy Spirit, the Kingdom of God, and the Father's will and purpose for mankind, as well as the many other laws and principles found in Scripture. Certainly, if we are going to be successful in sharing or defending our beliefs, we must first fully understand them ourselves. Have we bought out the time and applied our mind meditatively in a study of God's Word so that we can effectively share it with others? Paul exhorted his young traveling companion, Timothy, "Do your best to present yourself to God as one approved, a worker who has no need to be ashamed, rightly handling the word of truth." (2 Tim. 2:15) On this, the following commentaries write,

> God bestows his approval on the one who exhibits truth, love, and godliness in daily living, and who correctly handles the word of truth. The false teachers were mishandling God's words, using them for their own benefit. Timothy was commissioned to handle the words of God correctly. All preaching should present the truth clearly, cutting through erroneous ideas or inaccurate opinions.[77]

> Third, this same workman (specifically, Timothy but by application today all believers) was to be accurate in delivering the message of truth. The truth is the gospel. Paul showed concern that Timothy would present the gospel without perverting or distorting it. He was not to be turned aside by disputes about words or mere empty prattle.[78]

> Paul develops this concept in the striking phrase ... Paul's use of [*epaischunomai, aischunomai,* and *aischune*] means "unashamed" in the sense that he does not need to be ashamed of his work. The participle orthotomounta qualifies [*ergates*] and together with the words that follow specifically describes how Timothy may be unashamed: by being a worker who handles accurately the word of truth.

---

[77] Knute Larson, I & II Thessalonians, I & II Timothy, Titus, Philemon, vol. 9, Holman New Testament Commentary (Nashville, TN: Broadman & Holman Publishers, 2000), 286.

[78] Thomas D. Lea and Hayne P. Griffin, 1, 2 Timothy, Titus, vol. 34, The New American Commentary (Nashville: Broadman & Holman Publishers, 1992), 215.

The material that this worker is to handle correctly is "the word of truth" ... Only when he handles it correctly will he be unashamed ... The rendering given in several of the modern translations, using a combination of the verb "handle" and some adverb such as "accurately" (NASB), "rightly" (RSV), or "correctly" (NIV), for the compound verb [*orthotomounta*] with the phrase "the word of truth" as the direct object captures this relationship quite well.[79]

If we are going to be "a worker who has no need to be ashamed, rightly handling the word of truth," we must not always rely on others as being more effective, when we are called upon to share or defend our beliefs. Yes, God expects each of us to be capable of supporting our hope with Scripture. We do not want to fall under those who Paul mentioned to Timothy, "always learning and never able to arrive at a knowledge of the truth." (2 Tim. 3:7) We do not want to remain a spiritual babe for our entire Christian life. What do we think of children, who never really grow up and live with their parents off and on for their entire life? When we think of the many different professions in life, such as medicine, law, science, engineer, mechanic and so on, we know that our hands are held throughout our education, but once in the real world, we are expected to be self-reliant. Even Paul said of himself, "When I was a child, I spoke like a child, I thought like a child, I reasoned like a child. When I became a man, I gave up childish ways." – 1 Corinthians 13:11.

If we ever expect to defend our hope effectively, i.e., the faith, we are going to have to study daily. This should not trouble us because it does not take hours every day, but at least 30 minutes or more. The amount that can be accomplished in 30 minutes a day, after 365 days, will be far more than we might have ever expected. A Christian should study the Bible (not just read) a minimum of thirty minutes a day, he should also prepare the lessons assigned for the Bible study at the church and any other service that allows him to prepare ahead of time. A Christian should participate in any comment sessions that are allowed at their particular church, as this gives them practice in effectively sharing biblical truths. Also, A Christian should attend every Christian meeting, as it offers them an opportunity to build others up. A Christian should share every new thing they learn in their personal studies with at least one new friend, which gives them practice at effectively communicating biblical truths. We must have a deep understanding of the biblical truths that we share and defend, which is going to be presented to all kinds of different persons. Our studying daily needs to be a time on the day when we will not be disturbed. We want to

---

[79] George W. Knight, The Pastoral Epistles: a Commentary on the Greek Text, New International Greek Testament Commentary (Grand Rapids, MI; Carlisle, England: W.B. Eerdmans; Paternoster Press, 1992), 411–412.

turn the phone off, and music, television, and meditatively go through God's Word. The daily study will be our greatest tool for helping us to share and defend the Word of God and our faith effectively. Paul counsels Titus and by extension us as well, "let our people learn to devote themselves to good works, so as to help cases of urgent need, and not be unfruitful." (Titus 3:14) If we are studying daily, preparing for meetings, answering at meetings, attending all meetings, sharing a new biblical truth with friends, we will be able to apply Paul's thoughts to the Colossians as well. He wrote, "Let your speech always be gracious, seasoned with salt, so that you may know how you ought to answer each person." – Colossians 4:6

Using the Bible to Defend Our Hope

It should be noted that many today hold back from sharing or defending their Christian faith. Those who do, tend to do so without using the Bible. If we want to defend our hope successfully, we need to have our Bible as the primary evidence of that hope. Our hope lies within God's Word, so we need to use God's Word to defend it. We must persuade with reason from God's Word, not from how we feel, think, or believe. We need to go from 'this is how I **feel**, to, 'this is what I **know**, and here are the Scriptural reasons as to why.' It should be, 'the Word of God says,' Paul wrote,' 'Jesus said,' 'God said,' not 'I feel,' 'I think,' or 'I believe.' It is our effective use of the Bible when we communicated biblical truths to others that are going to convince the right-hearted ones of the truth and the way. One way that we will become more skilled is by our using our Bible at every opportunity: in our personal study of course, in sharing new truths with friends, and especially in looking up every Scripture that is cited in our religious services. Another way is to start paying attention to how commentaries and other study tools, as well as our pastors, elders tie Scriptures together contextually to establish their biblical point. If you were going to share the hope of salvation, could you walk a listener through 5-10 Scriptures that would paint a picture of that hope? Will our listener tell a friend of what they learned, and say, "He straight to his Bible and showed it to me directly!"

If we are sharing or defending biblical truths, we must do so correctly, persuasively, and in such a way that it is easy to grasp. This means that we know it well ourselves, and we have prepared well by communicating in more relaxed moments, which made us better communicators. For example, can we explain the resurrection hope at this very moment to another if they asked? Will our explanation be from the Bible? Will it be what the author meant by the words he used? Will it be persuasive? Will it be easy to follow and understand? If not, then, how can we honestly say we have a resurrection hope? Is there not irony that many young girls can tell you everything about Taylor Swift, but little if anything about their heavenly Father? The same is true of adult males, who can tear a car apart blindfolded but cannot string along a handful of verses that defend their resurrection hope. And yes, adult females have an immense amount of knowledge about subject matters that interest them, yet likely cannot support their resurrection hope any better. The above is a bit of a stereotype, which is noted, but it makes the point that we prepare for worldly things with far more vigor than we prepare to share and defend the faith.

If we are going to have any success in defending our Christian faith, we must be able to overcome the objections of others. We will find that the same objections are repeatedly used. Therefore, we will eventually, be able to overcome the standard objections easily. However, a couple of words of caution. First, we do not want to become complacent in our response to common objections; because the listener needs to feel as though they are getting an emotionally involved response, not some automatize, robotic response as if we feel like, 'here we go again.' Second, do not be complacent in thinking that every objection is going to be the common ones. If someone has an objection that we have never addressed, just simply say, "you raise a very good point, and the next time we speak, I will give you a logical and reasonable answer." When we research his objection, do so to the point that we know it inside and out. Moreover, be aware that 99 percent of all Bible difficulties have logical, reasonable answers. On this, R. A. Torrey writes, "Humbly. Recognize the limitations of your own mind and knowledge, and do not for a moment imagine that there is no solution just because you have found none. There is, in all probability, a very simple solution, even when you can find no solution at all."[80] In the end, there are answers, so meditate on the objection that has been raised, search through the literature, looking for Scripture and arguments to refute the objection in defense of the faith. Out of many thousands of Bible difficulties that have answers as to why they are, in fact, Bible difficulties and not errors, mistakes or contradictions, there are but a handful that has yet to be answered. This does not mean there is no answer, just that the information needed may be lacking, or it is something we will have to wait on until a greater mind comes along, or until the second coming of Christ. However, actually, if science had answers to many thousands of issues, but only a few remained unanswered, we would never hear the end of it. It is amazing that we have what we have considering we are dealing with a book where parts of it were penned 2,000 years ago while other parts were written 3,500 years ago.

As a proclaimer and defender of the faith, always be on the alert for points that can be used to overcome objections that we have heard, or

---

[80] http://www.christianpublishers.org/handling-bible-difficulties

what logically sounds like an objection one might raise. Whether we are studying a book, working on our Bible reading with a commentary or sitting in a pew listening to a talk from our elder or pastor, have our mind attuned to such things. Say, we are sitting at church, the pastor or elder makes an excellent point that overcomes a particular Bible objection (The Bible is not practical for our day, or there are so many different interpretations, who can know the truth), so we write it down in out notebook, because, yes, we have a notebook and pen. This will further implant the point in our mind. Now, we take it a step further. Find three different people after the meeting and say, "I really enjoyed what the pastor or elder had to say about the objection that the Bible is not practical for our day." Then, we should proceed to reiterate what was said in our own words. This will further embed it in our mind. Our notebook can be used for all kinds of notes at the meetings or during our personal study, but if we take notes on some objection or a Bible difficulty of some sort, highlight it a particular color. Why? We do this because we will also have another notebook that is specifically for Bible difficulties and Bible objections, so we have prepared and refutations. In this special notebook, leave the first few pages blank, as it will serve as our table of content. We can number our pages, so in the front, we can write down a phrase that will tell us what the issue is and the page on which it can be found.

The Third Obstacle to Our Being an Effective Evangelist

The **third greatest obstacle** is **Satan the Devil and his demon army.** Yes, they are so powerful that one demon could kill hundreds of thousands of humans in very short order. That is why true Christians receive a hedge placed around them by God, protecting them from Satan and the demons. Yes, God's servants receive special protection from this powerful force. (Job 1-2) The only way to weaken that protection is to violate your conscience repeatedly, toy with demonic activities, like horror movies, rap, and heavy metal music, games like the wigi-board or dungeons and dragons. However, we also weaken our protection from God when we repeatedly involve ourselves in the desires of the flesh. Below is a list by Paul, which covers the prominent works of the flesh, but it is not exhaustive. However, notice that he ends his list with the phrase, "and things like these." If we are carrying out a work of the flesh not listed and we think all is well because it is not on the list, we are sadly mistaken, because Paul includes all works of the flesh with the phrase, "and things like these."

Our human imperfections and the world that caters to them is with us 24/7. True, we can get control over our vessel by putting on the new personality, gaining the mind of Christ, and the help of Holy Spirit. However, it does not take much to drift away (Heb. 2:1), draw away (Heb. 3:12-13), fall away (Heb. 6:6), become sluggish (Heb. 6:12), shrink back from Christian responsibilities (Heb. 10.39), tire out (Heb. 12:3), refuse

(Heb. 12:25), or become hardened through deceptive powers (Gal. 6:9). We just need to entertain the wrong thoughts too long, without dismissing them, and then we are on our way. (James 1:14-15) Now, as far as Satan goes, Peter warns us in the extreme, to "be sober; be on the alert. Your adversary the devil walks around like a roaring lion, looking for someone to devour." (1 Pet. 5:8)

Paul also said that we are to,

Ephesians 6:11-12 Updated American Standard Version (UASV)

[11] Put on the full armor of God, so that you will be able to stand firm against the schemes of the devil. [12] For our struggle[81] is not against flesh and blood, but against the rulers, against the powers, against the world-rulers of this darkness, against the wicked spirit forces in the heavenly places.

Threefold Assistance in Our Being an Effective Evangelist

There is a threefold defense against this threefold opposition to our being an effective evangelist for God. **First,** we have **the Word of God,** which should come in the way of literal translations, like the Updated American Standard Version, the New American Standard Bible, and the English Standard Version. God gave us this special revelation to guide us through this wicked time. It has the power to make us stronger spiritually, as well as fortify us to accomplish his will and purposes. The apostle Paul tells us, "For the word of God is living and active and sharper than any two-edged sword, and piercing as far as the division of soul and spirit, of both joints and marrow, and able to judge the thoughts and intentions of the heart." –Hebrews 4:12.

The Bible should be read daily, in conjunction with CPH's recommended Bible reading program.[82] We also need to use our Bible in all of our religious meetings. If a Scripture is being read, we need to look it up. We also need to use our Bible in our ministry, meaning that we need to formulate texts that can help us to teach others the good news of the Kingdom.

Deuteronomy 17:19 Updated American Standard Version (UASV)

[19] And you shall come to the Levitical priests and to the judge who is in office in those days, and you shall consult them, and they will declare to you the verdict in the case.

As we work our way through the Bible in our Bible reading program, let us not rush, but make sure we understand the author's intended meaning, and how we can apply that in our lives, as well as share it with

---

[81] Lit., "wrestling."
[82] http://www.christianpublishers.org/the-new-bible-study

others. We should be able to see our walking with God, come to life through the historical accounts found all throughout Scripture.

Joshua 1:7-8 Updated American Standard Version (UASV)

⁷ Only be strong and very courageous, being careful to do according to all the law that Moses my servant commanded you; do not turn from it to the right or to the left, so that you may have success wherever you go. ⁸ This Book of the Law shall not depart from your mouth, but you shall meditate on it day and night, so that you may be careful to do according to all that is written in it; for then you will make your way prosperous, and then you will have good success.

Below in Psalm 1:1-3, you will notice in verse 1 that there is a progression of intimacy through walking in the counsel of the wicked, to standing with sinners, to sitting with scoffers. Each level is a sign of spending more time with, being more deeply involved. We should not be involved with any of these three because this would never be in harmony with a Christian, who is walking with God. After that, the Psalmist in verse 2 helps us to appreciate where our delight is found, the law of Jehovah, to which we read and study in a meditative way, day and night, which simply means on a regular basis. Truly, verse 3 helps us to appreciate the result of avoiding certain ones and cultivating a love for God's Word, endurance and a strong spiritual health. If we follow the counsel of verses 1-2, we will be able to weather any storm that may come upon us. Think, this is but three verses out of over 31,000 verses, which offer us the very knowledge of God.

Psalm 1:1-3 Updated American Standard Version (UASV)

¹ Blessed is the man
   who walks not in the counsel of the wicked,
nor stands in the way of sinners,
   nor sits in the seat of scoffers;
² but his delight is in the law of Jehovah,
   and on his law he meditates day and night.

³ He is like a tree
   planted by streams of water
that yields its fruit in its season,
   and its leaf does not wither.
In all that he does, he prospers.

Second, along with God's Word, are some of the best **Bible study tools** as well as the **Christian congregation**. Paul tells the Ephesians, "Look carefully then how you walk, not as unwise but as wise, making the best use of the time, because the days are evil." (Eph. 5:15-16) Moreover, the Apostle Paul exhorted "let us consider how to stir up one another to love and good works, not neglecting to meet together, as is the habit of some, but encouraging one another, and all the more as you see the Day drawing near." (Heb. 10:24-25) We need to have a personal Bible study for at least thirty minutes a day, every day of the week. Moreover, we need to prepare for the Christian meetings, so as to participate in them, whether it be answering at the Bible study classes or looking up Scripture and taking notes at those with lectures.

Third, we have to be effectively sharing God's Word with others. It is our sharing offensively and defensively that will keep us in battle mode, always prepared to defend the hope that we have, always taking in the very knowledge of God on a more deeper level, the every Word that is Spirit-inspired, meaning always taking in and applying Spirit inspired, inerrant Word of God. The apostle Paul told the Galatians that if we can walk by the 'walk by the Spirit, we will not carry out the desire of the flesh.' How are we to walk by the Spirit? We do so by taking the Spirit-inspired Word into our minds so that we are inundated mentally by it, so that it becomes our way of thinking, and to do otherwise would trigger a warning from our Christian conscience.

Galatians 5:16-26 Updated American Standard Version (UASV)

16 But I say, walk by the Spirit, and you will not carry out the desire of the flesh. 17 For the desires of the flesh are against the Spirit, and the desires of the Spirit are against the flesh, for these are opposed to each other, so that you may not do the things you want to do. 18 But if you are led by the Spirit, you are not under the law. 19 Now the works of the flesh are evident, which are: sexual immorality, impurity, sensuality, 20 idolatry, sorcery, enmity, strife, jealousy, fits of anger, rivalries, dissensions, divisions, 21 envy, drunkenness, orgies, and things like these. I warn you, as I warned you before, that those who do such things will not inherit the kingdom of God. 22 But the fruit of the Spirit is love, joy, peace, patience, kindness, goodness, faithfulness, 23 gentleness, self-control; against such things there is no law. 24 And those who belong to Christ Jesus have crucified the flesh with its passions and desires.

25 If we live by the Spirit, let us also walk by the Spirit. 26 Let us not become conceited, provoking one another, envying one another.

Those who follow the flesh will reap the results of such a course by having unattractive fruits. On the other hand, those who follow the lead of the Spirit will have fruitage that is attractive and beneficial for themselves, family, congregation, friends, and neighbors. One thing that we have to realize by looking at other related texts is, these fruits are not the results of our efforts, but rather they are the consequence of having an active faith in Christ, which makes us receptive to them. In addition, it is the fruitage of the Spirit, which is going to sustain us through a lifetime of proclaiming the good news, teaching the Word and making disciples.

While there are many enemies against or in opposition to our walking with God aright, the greatest is our own human imperfection, followed the world of humankind that is alienated from God, as well as Satan the Devil and his demon army. So too, many things can keep us spiritually strong, but the most effective are the Word of God (preparing for Christian meetings and personal study), regular attendance and participation at Christian meetings, followed by effectively sharing our faith.

Therefore, we must trust in God by applying his Word with conviction in our lives, especially in being bold as we go about sharing the Word in these difficult times, just as was true of the apostle Paul and Barnabas in the first century. As these two, brought the Word of God to Iconium, their evangelism created a sharp division of feelings, thoughts and some opposition. On this, Kenneth O. Gangel writes, "As in Pisidian Antioch, the opposition came not from Gentiles but from unbelieving Jews. Luke uses poignant language to describe what happened–stirring up the Gentiles, the Jews **poisoned their minds**, literally 'caused their minds to think evil.' Not only against Paul and Barnabas but against all believers there (**the brothers**). This time, rather than shaking off the dust of the city, Paul and Barnabas evidently decided that the persecution actually gave them a good reason to stay a **considerable time** in Iconium. They spoke boldly for the Lord (Luke surely intends us to understand "Jesus" here), and he confirmed the message through miracles (*semeia kai terata*). All this took place in Galatia, so we can understand this ministry in light of the Galatian letter. There Paul tells us that these mighty works of the Spirit certified that God approved his gospel (Gal. 3:4–5). Luke uses an interesting phrase–**the message of his grace**–to describe the gospel. The linking of the message with the accompanying miracle reminds us of Hebrews 2:1–4. Signs and wonders in Acts remind us of the transitional nature of this book. Barnhouse puts it well:"

> These signs and wonders were specially given to the apostles and early Christian church workers because there was no written New Testament as yet. Not a line of the New Testament had been written at this point, and there was no solid authority to which the apostles could point and say, "See, we're preaching truth. You can check it in the Word of God!" There was no completed Word of God. So God enabled the apostles to perform wonders and signs to authenticate their ministry, but

these wonders and signs would fade as God's Word came into being (Barnhouse, 126).[83]

We must remember as the United States of America, the last bastion of religious freedom on earth fades into an atheistic, socialist country, opposition to our work, as evangelists will grow, as we draw ever closer to the second coming of Christ. Nevertheless, just know that "this gospel of the kingdom will be proclaimed in the whole inhabited earth for a testimony to all the nations, and then the end will come." (Matt. 24:14, LEB) Each of us can do our part by evangelizing our communities, making sure everyone has an opportunity to hear, knowing that as the end draws near almost none will listen.

On what Foundation Should Our Evangelism Be Based?

Is our foundation based on the Word of God or on human wisdom? We should consider the counsel that Paul gave his young traveling companion, Timothy. "You, however, continue in the things you have learned and were persuaded to believe, knowing from whom you have learned them, [15] and that from infancy[84] you have known the sacred writings, which are able to make you wise for salvation through trust[85] in Christ Jesus. [16] All Scripture is inspired by God and profitable for teaching, for reproof, for correction, for training in righteousness; [17] so that the man of God may be fully competent, equipped for every good work."

Clearly, when we consider the Gospels, all Jesus said therein comes to about a three to four-hour talk, and he quoted or referred to over 120 Scriptures. Of course, in a three-and-a-half-year ministry, Jesus said far more than that, but it gives us insight into how much the Son of God himself depended on Scripture. The apostle Paul is one of the greatest Christian teachers of all time. At a synagogue of the Jews in Thessalonica, "according to Paul's custom, he went to them, and for three Sabbaths **reasoned with them from the Scriptures, explaining and proving** that it was necessary that the Christ had to suffer and rise again from the dead, and saying, 'This Jesus whom I am proclaiming to you is the Christ.'" – Acts 17:1-3.

What was the result of Paul's "reasoned with them from the Scriptures, explaining and proving"? The account says, "Some of them were persuaded

---

83 Kenneth O. Gangel, *Acts*, vol. 5, Holman New Testament Commentary (Nashville, TN: Broadman & Holman Publishers, 1998), 231.

84 *Brephos* is "the period of time when one is very young–'childhood (probably implying a time when a child is still nursing), infancy." – GELNTBSD

85 *Pisteuo* is "to believe to the extent of complete trust and reliance—'to believe in, to have confidence in, to have faith in, to trust, faith, trust.'" – GELNTBSD

and joined Paul and Silas, as did a great many of the devout Greeks and not a few of the leading women." – Acts 17:4.

While we can proclaim and teach anything that is within the Scriptures, what should be our primary message? Since we are to follow in the footsteps of Jesus, we might consider his commission. On one occasion, Jesus "departed and went into a desolate place. And the people sought him and came to him, and they tried to keep him from going away from them. But he said to them, "I must **preach the <u>kingdom of God</u>** to the other cities also, for I **was sent for** <u>this purpose</u>." (Lu 4:43) In fact, in reference to the last days, Jesus said, "And this gospel of the kingdom will be proclaimed in all the inhabited earth[86] as a testimony to all the nations, and then the end will come." – Matthew 24:14.

Returning to the apostle Paul, we see this was an emphasis in his proclaiming and teaching. Here again, Paul "entered the synagogue and for three months **spoke boldly, reasoning** and **persuading** them **about the <u>kingdom of God</u>**. When Paul was in Rome, "they came to him at his lodging in greater numbers; and he **expounded** to them, **testifying about <u>the kingdom of God</u>** and **trying to persuade** them concerning Jesus both from the Law of Moses and from the Prophets, from morning till evening." For two whole years in Rome, Paul was "**proclaiming the <u>kingdom of God</u>** and **teaching** about the Lord Jesus Christ **with all boldness** and without hindrance." – Acts 19:8; 28:23, 31.

Using God's Word Skillfully

The apostle Paul sought to motivate those who listened to him so that they would act upon the Gospel. Note his words to the Thessalonians, he writes, "for our gospel did not come to you in word only, but also in power and in the Holy Spirit and with full conviction; just as you know what kind of men we proved to be among you for your sake. And you became imitators of us and of the Lord, for you received the word in much affliction, with joy inspired by the Holy Spirit, so that you became an example to all the believers in Macedonia and in Achaia." (1 Thess. 1:5-7) Paul not only sought to appeal to the mind, that is, the seat of thought, ideas, and perceptions, but also to heart, namely, the seat of motivation. We return to Paul's defense before King Agrippa, as he handles the Word of God about Moses and the prophets aright. – 2 Timothy 2:15.

Paul was aware the Agrippa was technically a Jew. Therefore, he appealed to Agrippa's knowledge of Judaism. Paul linked his witness in such a way, to deny it was to deny Moses and the prophets. Paul said to all standing there, 'To this day I have had the help that comes from God, and

---

[86] Or *in the whole world*

so I stand here testifying both to small and great, saying nothing but what the prophets and Moses said would come to pass. [That is,] the Christ must suffer, and that, by being the first to rise from the dead, he would proclaim light both to the people and to the Gentiles." (Acts 26:22-23) Now, let us look at this exchange to see how Paul not only guides people to the truth but also leads them in such a way, if they reject it, they are rejecting their beliefs or their method of reasoning. Modern day Christian Philosophers and Christian apologists, such as the late Ronald Nash, John M. Frame, John Lennox, Alister McGrath, Sean and Josh McDowell, Ravi Zacharias, Norman L. Geisler and William Lane Craig, among many others, use philosophical arguments to help guide those with college and university degrees into the truth. In logic, reason and philosophy, arguments are used to persuade those who also use logic, reason and philosophy for accepting a conclusion. In other words, they use their own tools against these from higher learning, to reject the logic, reason and philosophical arguments, if sound, is to reject their own tools of the trade.

Acts 26:24 Updated American Standard Version (UASV)

24 And as he was saying these things in his defense, Festus said with a loud voice, "Paul, you are out of your mind; your great learning is turning you to madness."

This statement by Festus really tied the hands of Agrippa. Even still, Paul left him with no means of escape or room to maneuver.

Acts 26:25-26 Updated American Standard Version (UASV)

25 But Paul said, "I am not out of my mind, most excellent Festus, but I am speaking true and rational words. 26 For the king knows about these things, and to him **I speak boldly**. For I am persuaded that none of these things has escaped his notice, for this has not been done in a corner.

Paul again appeals to Agrippa's vanity, but also his knowledge of Scripture. However, he is also aware that he has just placed Agrippa in a spot. Agrippa was in trouble no matter with whom he sided. If he rejected what Moses and the prophets said, he would be dismissed as a Jewish believer. However, if he said that Paul was correct, he would be viewed as siding with an apostle of Christ Jesus and making himself a Christian. Moreover, to side with Paul would mean he agreed with the person Festus called, 'out of his mind and had gone mad.' Therefore, Paul did not allow Agrippa to remain in this uncomfortable position for long, so he answered his own question.

Acts 26:27 Updated American Standard Version (UASV)

27 King Agrippa, do you believe the prophets? I know that you believe."

Agrippa saw a great mind at work here, and he could see how effective Paul's reasoning skill was. It moved Agrippa and touched his heart. He did not fear giving Paul a truthful answer, which seems to demonstrate a reciprocation of the same respect and honor that the apostle Paul had shown him.

Acts 26:28 Updated American Standard Version (UASV)

28 And Agrippa said to Paul, "In a short time you will persuade me to become a Christian."

It is true, Agrippa was not moved to become a Christian, but Paul evidenced that "the word of God is living and active and sharper than any two-edged sword, and piercing as far as the division of soul and spirit, of both joints and marrow, and able to judge the thoughts and intentions of the heart." (Heb. 4:12) We should also notice that Paul's defense included both proclamation and persuasion. It is this approach as he "rightly handling the word of truth" which allowed him to bring many congregations of Christians into the fold of Christianity. We see this very thing in his establishing the congregation in Thessalonica.

Acts 17:1-4 Updated American Standard Version (UASV)

1 Now when they had passed through Amphipolis and Apollonia, they came to Thessalonica, where there was a synagogue of the Jews. 2 And according to Paul's custom, he went to them, and for three Sabbaths **reasoned with them from the Scriptures,** 3 **explaining** and **proving** that it was necessary that the Christ had to suffer and rise again from the dead, and saying, "This Jesus whom I am proclaiming to you is the Christ." 4 And **some of them were persuaded** and joined Paul and Silas, as did a great many of the devout Greeks and not a few of the leading women.

We can see that Paul was persuasive, as he reasoned with them from the Scriptures, explaining and proving that Jesus was the Christ. In the end, Paul was able to establish one of the earliest Christian congregations. We too must become more skilled in the art of persuasion as we go about sharing the Word of God. If we can, we will find the idea of proclaiming and persuading not so overwhelming, as we too go about adding to the congregation of God.

1 Timothy 2:3-4 Updated American Standard Version (UASV)

3 This is good, and it is acceptable in the sight of God our Savior, 4 who desires all men to be saved and to come to an accurate knowledge[87] of truth.

---

[87] *Epignosis* is a strengthened or intensified form of *gnosis* (*epi*, meaning "additional"), meaning, "true," "real," "full," "complete" or "accurate," depending upon the context. Paul and Peter alone use *epignosis*.

Apollos Speaks Boldly in Ephesus

The first-century Christian, Apollos, was to talk about God's Word. Each Christian today certainly desires to be able to espouse God and his Word as we are 'always prepared to make a defense[88] to anyone who asks us for a reason for the hope that is in us. (1 Pet. 3:15) We want to always be ready to give an answer from God's Word to sincere questions (Col. 4:6), which is quite rewarding to know we are following in the footsteps of Christ, Paul, Apollos, and the first-century Christians. Our joy grows ever greater as we are able to use God's Word skillfully, efficiently, as we watch the light of understanding grow in the eyes of those with which we speak. Notice Apollos' boldness, how he was fervent in spirit, as he was speaking and teaching the things concerning Jesus accurately.

Acts 18:24-28 Updated American Standard Version (UASV)

[24] Now a certain Jew named Apollos, a native of Alexandria, an eloquent man, arrived in Ephesus; and he was well versed in the Scriptures. [25] This man had been orally instructed in the way of the Lord; and being fervent in spirit, he was speaking and teaching accurately the things concerning Jesus, being acquainted only with the baptism of John; [26] and this man began to speak out boldly in the synagogue. But when Priscilla and Aquila heard him, they took him aside and explained to him the way of God more accurately. [27] And when he wanted to go across to Achaia, the brethren encouraged him and wrote to the disciples to welcome him; and when he had arrived, he greatly helped those who had believed through grace, [28] for he powerfully refuted the Jews in public, demonstrating by the Scriptures that Jesus was the Christ.

Helping Spiritually

It is not only our goal to win arguments, to fill heads with knowledge, but also to help people spiritually. Many people that we hope to speak with have had many discussions with Christians over the years. They have read books about God, the Bible, even the Christian faith because they have a spiritual need of which they are unaware. Over these years, they likely have come across aggressive Christians; persons who have beat them with the Bible, and misinformed Christians espousing untruths, not biblical truths. What these now need is a respectful Bible discussion where they can get their pent-up questions answered by a loving disciple of Christ.

When we come to someone with the Word of God in hand, but also a sincere, loving, Christlike spirit of humility, this adds a persuasive power

---

[88] Or *argument*, or *explanation*

that he may have never experienced. We want to be sensitive to his experiences with other Christians prior to us, books that they may have read, or relatives they have dealt with, and as we fulfill his spiritual needs by way of God's Word. Even if he is a new Christian, having just come to the faith, he can be prepared to use God's Word as well. At first, he might be shy, timid, or hesitant about sharing God's Word. However, if he regularly prepares for and attends Christian meetings, as well as have a consistent personal Bible study at home daily, it will not be long before he has a deeper knowledge of the Scriptures.

THE BOOK OF JAMES
CPH New Testament Commentary

An Apologetic and Background Exposition of the Holy Scriptures (UASV)

Edward D. Andrews &
Brent A. Calloway

Bibliography

Anders, M. (1999). *Holman New Testament Commentary: vol. 8, Galatians-Colossians* . Nashville, TN: Broadman & Holman Publishers.

Barclay, W. (2002). *The Letters to the Galatians and Ephesians, The New Daily Study Bible.* Louisville, KY; London: Westminster John Knox Press.

Brand, C., Draper, C., & Archie, E. (2003). *Holman Illustrated Bible Dictionary: Revised, Updated and Expanded.* Nashville, TN: Holman.

Bratcher, R. G., & Nida, E. A. (1993). *A Handbook on Paul's Letter to the Ephesians, UBS Handbook Series.* New York: United Bible Societies.

Bromiley, G. W. (1986). *The International Standard Bible Encyclopedia (Vol. 1-4).* Grand Rapids, MI: William B. Eerdmans Publishing Co.

Elwell, W. A., & Beitzel, B. J. (1988). *Baker Encyclopedia of the Bible.* Grand Rapids, MI: Baker Book House.

Elwell, W. A., & Comfort, P. W. (2001). *Tyndale Bible Dictionary.* Wheaton: Tyndale House Publishers.

Hodges, C. (1994). *(1994) Commentary on the Epistle to the Ephesians.* Grand Rapids, MI: Wm B. Eerdmans Publishing Co.

MacArthur, J. (1986). *The MacArthur New Testament Commentary: Ephesians.* Chicago: Moody Press.

Mounce, W. D. (2006). *Mounce's Complete Expository Dictionary of Old & New Testament Words.* Grand Rapids, MI: Zondervan.

Muddiman, J. (2001). *The Epistle to the Ephesians, Black's New Testament Commentary.* London: Continuum.

O'Brien, P. T. (1999). *The Letter to the Ephesians, The Pillar New Testament Commentary.* Grand Rapids, MI: W.B. Eerdmans Publishing Co.

Ryle, J. C. (2001). *Holiness.* USA: Charles Nolan Publishers.

Snodgrass, K. (1996). *Ephesians, The NIV Application Commentary.* Grand Rapids, MI: Zondervan.

Swanson, J. (1997). *Dictionary of Biblical Languages with Semantic Domains: Greek (New Testament).* Oak Harbor: Logos Research Systems.

Vine, W. E., Unger, M. F., & White Jr., W. (1996). *Vine's Complete Expository Dictionary of Old and New Testament Words.* Nashville, TN: T. Nelson.

Whiston, W. (1987). *The Works of Josephus.* Peabody, MA: Hendrickson.

Wood, D. R. (1996). *New Bible Dictionary (Third Edition).* Downers Grove: InterVarsity Press.